We Will
Never Forget

Eyewitness Accounts of the
Bombing of the
Oklahoma City
Federal Building

Jim Ross & Paul Myers

EAKIN PRESS ★ Austin, Texas

FIRST EDITION

Copyright © 1996
By Jim Ross and Paul Myers

Published in the United States of America
By Eakin Press
An Imprint of Sunbelt Media Inc.
P.O. Drawer 90159 ★ Austin, TX 78709-0159

ISBN 1-57168-081-0

2   3   4   5   6   7   8   9

Cover photo: Courtesy David Allen

To the Families

Contents

Preface

The terrorist attack on the Alfred P. Murrah Federal Building in Oklahoma City on April 19, 1995, left 169 men, women, and children dead, an equal number of families wrecked, and hundreds more wounded. The building itself, nine stories of glass, steel and concrete, was virtually demolished. Also nearly destroyed were the offices of the Oklahoma Water Resources Board, the Athenian Restaurant, and the Journal Record building, all located across the street. Less than a block away, the YMCA sustained heavy damage, as did the Regency Tower, an apartment high-rise. Throughout the area, dozens of businesses had doors blown from hinges and walls knocked flat. Parked cars, riddled by shrapnel, exploded in flames, and city streets for miles were sprayed with shattered glass. All of this happened within three seconds of the detonation of a Ryder rental truck stuffed with explosive fertilizer by a vengeful sociopath. It was an act that stunned the world.

The immediate reaction was as unpredictable as the bombing. Panic by victims and a chaotic rescue attempt never materialized. It may have been the sheer shock of it, or an instinctive, collective focus on the urgent need to get as many survivors as possible out of the building. Citizen witnesses, police officers in the area, and arriving firemen assaulted the smoldering ruins with a desperate determination and total disregard for their own safety. As the first victims were carried out, medical personnel rushing toward the disaster had arrived to receive them. On their heels were the organized rescue teams, already dispatched and operational under the direction of law enforcement and fire department brass. At local hospitals, surgical teams were standing ready when the first sirens screamed into their driveways.

From across the nation, helping hands scrambled to get to Oklahoma. Rescuers and volunteers came from as far away as New York, Florida, California, and Washington, and from many other states as well. They set up canteens, hauled in food, gathered supplies, and untiringly dug through the building's crushed remains until ordered to quit. Closer to home, construction workers dispatched from union locals literally risked their lives shoring up the sagging building to make it safe for the rescue effort. Charitable organizations swung into action and remained on duty around the clock, and throughout the ordeal, local clergy and counselors ministered to apprehensive families as they bravely stood vigil, day after endless day. Thousands of cards and letters, mostly from children, came in a flash flood of love from around the world.

These pages tell the stories of the rescue workers, doctors and nurses, survivors, family members, and volunteers who found themselves unexpectedly thrust into one of the worst nightmares in our country's history. Their words are powerful, poignant, raw, chilling. By sharing their experiences, they have not only helped to create a permanent record, they have demonstrated that humankind is still rooted in goodness and compassion. For that, we salute them.

JIM ROSS & PAUL MYERS
Oklahoma City, Oklahoma

Acknowledgments

Our commitment to seeing this project in print could not have been realized without the help and support of many friends and colleagues. Fellow Oklahoma writers Deborah Bouziden, Jan May, Taprina Milburn, Suzi Shoemake, Allison Thompson, and Jan Vassar were responsible for seeking out dozens of the stories that fill these pages and, quite simply, without their efforts there would be no book. Our good friend Mike Brake, chief writer for Oklahoma Governor Frank Keating, was a valued resource whose door was always open and whose wise counsel was more than once put to good use. Ginny Myers, Rachel Posey, and Robert Hart answered without hesitation the call to type and proofread parts of the manuscript, and writer Terri Branson, who unwittingly became our full-time editorial assistant, volunteered her computer wizardry and countless hours at the keyboard to produce the final manuscript, on time. A special thanks is also due Abbie Fiser and Anna Myers for their encouragement and editorial advice. To all of you, we are truly and deeply grateful.

Finally, it is only because of the individuals whose lives were suddenly and forever changed on April 19, 1995, that this narrative exists. The willingness of so many of them to revisit the event with pen and paper and then entrust to strangers their private thoughts in the wake of their own suffering teaches all of us something about the human heart. God bless you all. You will never be forgotten.

You have lost too much, but you have not lost every-thing. And you have certainly not lost America, for we will stand with you for as many tomorrows as it takes.

PRESIDENT BILL CLINTON
Oklahoma City
April 23, 1995

April 19, 1995
9:02 A.M.

Oklahoma City Police and
Fire Department Dispatch Excerpts
(D is for Dispatcher)

POLICE:

(unknown unit) . . . there's an explosion downtown!

D: 10-20?

(unknown unit) He just said there's some kind of explosion downtown.

D: Can you give me a location?

—an explosion downtown! We need help! Get me the fire department!

It's about Broadway and Fifth.

D: Okay.

34, I heard the explosion. I can see it. There's several of us out here. Don't know what it is.

(unknown unit) It's about, uh, Fourth and Broadway, back west.

Adam 24's en route.

30, en route.

—it may be the Federal Building, I'm not sure.

FIRE DEPARTMENT:

316 to dispatch, this explosion's at Fifth and uh, Robinson. This is the Oklahoma Water Resources Board. Clear?

D: Headquarters clear, Fifth and North Robinson.

600 to dispatch, what have you got runnin' on this alarm?

D: . . . 600, we haven't been able to dispatch anybody yet.

(unknown unit) . . . we have visible smoke, looks like the roof has uh, the roof has collapsed.

601 establishing command at Sixth and Harvey . . .

(unknown unit) . . . multiple alarm sounded. Start a second and a third and a fourth. The Federal Building . . . we've got a lot of people here.

D: Engine 51, Engine 1 . . . Truck 1, Truck 6, Truck 5, Squad 1, 601 . . . northwest five and Robinson, northwest five and Robinson. Run number 4543, at 9:03.

POLICE:

146, we got glass and windows everywhere!

D: Okay, 52, 44 and 34 en route. Was there another one?

— need an ambulance —

20's goin' 97, I'm going off the air.

(unknown unit) — headquarters, you might start us as many EMSA units as possible.

There's a lot of injuries.

Adam 24 headquarters, we're 97, we got damage and injuries all up and down Broadway.

— got fire, everybody.

Adam 24 to headquarters. I need, uh, help in front of the YMCA. We got several injuries.

FIRE DEPARTMENT:

This is 600. The whole front of the Federal Building is gone — all floors to the roof.

— we need a pumper over here on, uh, Robinson. We could put out those car fires and cut down on the black smoke.

— I need another truck, Fifth and Harvey. We're still having some explosions in this fire.

POLICE:

— I've got six, seven people down! In the 100 block of Northwest Fifth.

D: EMSA's been advised.

— north side of the building —

D: Your signal's breaking.

— ten people buried under rubble —

D: Adam 38, are you on the north side of the Federal Building with people buried?

I'm on the east side of the Federal Building, east side!

Be advised . . . there's a children's center and we need the fire department up here quick.

— I've got two down in the 100 block that are not moving. The ones I can I'm gonna transport to a hospital. I've got about six.

— people trapped on this situation, fifth floor.

FIRE DEPARTMENT:

(unknown unit) . . . send me about three more companies, there are reports of twenty people trapped in this building.

—we need the water department, water

department, shut-off, we've got high water rising quickly.

D: Clear on water department.

(unknown unit) Inform EMSA, we need medical supplies.

Harvey division to any medical command: We need some help here on Fifth Street real bad. Right now!

316 to dispatch . . . need numerous crews over here . . . many people trapped on the second floor. We need extrication crews!

POLICE:

— people in the building!

D: Go ahead.

— We need equipment. We've got people on the second floor jumpin' out windows. We need ladders and firemen here quick.

— we got 'em trying to climb down on sheets. I know they got a lot going on, they need a ladder over here, though.

FIRE DEPARTMENT:

(unknown unit) . . . we have two patients critical. We are out of supplies.

City police to city fire: Medical coordinator contact dispatch immediately.

(unknown unit) . . . we definitely need some more manpower!

PART

I

Desperate
Hours

I saw an elderly white woman carrying a black baby. A young black woman ran toward her screaming, "My baby! Is that my baby?" When she got within five feet of the child and saw its face, she turned west and continued running, screaming, "Where's my baby? Where's my baby?"

Baltazar Morales is in charge of computer operations at Oklahoma City's 9-1-1 center.

At the exact time I heard and felt the blast, I was on the telephone talking to Major Ricky Williams of the Fire Department. Major Williams was asking me to prepare a report on the number and locations of all fire incidents involving explosions in the period since July 1994.

∽

Police Officer Terrance Yeakey arrived at the Federal Building within two minutes of the blast.

I was looking for a suspect in a stabbing when I heard and felt what I thought was an earthquake. Within seconds I heard the radio broadcast, so I turned on my lights and siren and rushed to the scene.

I didn't see any people near the building, so I hurried to the burning cars in the lot across the street to see if anybody there needed help. The fire was so intense I couldn't get close. It wasn't until I turned back that I actually saw what had happened. I called Dispatch and told them the whole north side of the Murrah Building was gone.

I ran into the building to look for survivors. I found a man against a wall not far inside the entrance. He couldn't stand. He said his name was Tom and he had been with a friend. I looked around and found a hand sticking out from underneath a collapsed wall. I felt for a pulse, but got none. I picked up Tom and turned to carry him out when I heard his friend call from under the rubble. Tom's throat had been cut wide open, so I went ahead and hustled him outside.

I ran back into the building and was able to uncover Tom's friend. Miraculously, he walked out. Again, I ran back inside. This time I had help. We carried out a woman with a deep gash on her leg. Next we found a man named Randy. All we could see was part of his face. He was completely buried. We couldn't tell where his arms or legs were.

We began lifting blocks of concrete off of Randy. He would tell us it hurt as we lifted the chunks one by one. I lifted a board off his face and part of his face peeled back.

Finally, we freed Randy and started to carry him out. Suddenly, the ground I was walking on gave way and I fell in a hole. I don't remember much after that. I remember lying in the ambulance beside Randy. He looked bad. He had a tube down his throat, and I didn't think he was going to make it. The next thing I remember, I was in the hospital with a back injury.

∽

Janet Brooks was at work in the Main Library, only two blocks from the Murrah Building.

I felt a gust of wind across my face and then the glass started coming in. I screamed and ran around the other side of the partition for cover. I saw Karen on the floor. I thought she had hit the deck for cover, too, and only later realized that she had been knocked down. We all had dazed looks on our faces, as we asked each other if we were okay. We heard someone yell for us to get out of the building. I grabbed my purse and headed out on Ruby's heels.

∽

OCFD Corporal Oliver Moore was assigned to drive Rescue Squad 1 on April 19. He arrived downtown at 9:04 A.M.

I slid the pole and ran into the alley behind the station. A towering column of smoke was rising above the street a few blocks east of us. Squad 1 loaded up and headed out. The sidewalks were crowded with people looking toward the smoke. When we topped the hill at the intersection of 5th and Dewey streets, I saw a layer of shattered glass covering the pavement for three blocks ahead of us.

At 5th and Harvey smoke billowed across the intersection. Everything to the south was obscured, so I turned north and parked at 6th Street, thinking the main damage was north of 5th. Recruit Timothy Goff and I attempted a ladder rescue of a woman trapped on the second floor of the restaurant adjacent to the Water Resources Board Building, but by the time we got to the alley with the ladder, another fireman had already helped her down.

Another victim was found in the same alley a little further east. The man was trapped under concrete and wire mesh. Part of the roof of the Journal Record Building had fallen on him. Using an ax and forcible entry tools, we were able to free him. He appeared to have a broken hip and an open compound fracture of one leg and ankle. He was lucky. That roof had fallen four floors. Nearby, cars were on fire. Beyond, through the diminishing smoke, I saw the front of the Federal Building for the first time. For about fifteen seconds I just stood there, dumbfounded.

∽

Carrie Hulsey is the police reporter for Oklahoma City radio station KTOK.

I was in the news car at the stoplight at 4th and Harvey, on the south side of the Murrah Building, when it blew. My car jumped off the ground and my ears started ringing. I remember seeing the colors of the stained glass from the windows of St. Joseph's Church flying toward my car. One minute and thirty seconds later I was on the air. That's when we began our wall-to-wall coverage.

∽

Oklahoma City Police Sergeant Kevin Thompson is with the Springlake Division.

I ran north on Robinson to the south side of the building. The first officers I saw were Sergeants Richard Williams and Keith Simonds. Keith was carrying a woman who looked very dead to me. Keith was covered in the woman's blood and Richard was soaked as if he had been under water. Keith laid her on the sidewalk where a fireman began first aid. The three of us stood in the middle of the street near an ambulance. As we pulled our gloves on, someone laid a small dead body next to us. I will never forget the sight of Richard leaning over this dead child and saying over and over, "Oh my God, Oh my God."

A few minutes later we entered the building. I gave Keith the small flashlight I always carry and I used my big flashlight. The basement was pitch black and in some places the chilly water was waist deep. We encountered some firemen freeing victims. Within minutes three females were located, all alive, but mostly buried. Junk was still falling down on us. A large block of concrete was hanging precariously over our heads. I told the fire captain to look up and as he did, he asked me what my name was. "Thompson," I told him, to which he replied, "Well, Thompson, if it falls and you make it out, tell them where my body is."

I continued to stare at that slab of concrete over our heads. I cannot describe the feeling. I turned and got sick to my stomach. Not because of what I was seeing, but more like a nervous sickness. I guess I thought I was going to die, so I told myself not to look up. After about an hour, we handed out our first freed lady. We handed the victims to citizens who were standing at ground level. Soon we handed out another lady who was pregnant. The fire captain was still on his knees talking to his trapped victim, and still waiting for some tools so he could get her out. As our search continued, we found several dead children.

∽

Ernestine Clark is director of development for the Metropolitan Library System.

I saw window blinds banging wildly and glass all over.

Lee Brawner yelled at me to "Get down! Get down!" We found our TV coordinator, Barbara Williams, on the third floor, injured and gray with shock. Lee lifted her up and yelled to the rest of us to evacuate the building.

I started running down the stairs of the library, aware that no one else was around. As I reached the first floor, I froze in shock. The main entrance doors were blown in. Even the frames were bent. For the first time I realized this was not just something that happened to the library.

We put Barbara on the curb in front of a fire hydrant. She was shivering. I roamed the sidewalk, stopping to ask people, "Do you have a blanket? Do you know someone with a blanket?" They all shook their heads, distracted. I looked up the hill to see what they were looking at, and found myself staring at the front of the Murrah Building, breathless. A single thought rushed into my head and repeated itself, over and over: "This is horrible, horrible!"

∞

Rick Martin was at work at the C. R. Anthony Co. building one block away from the blast. He later worked as a volunteer during the search and recovery effort.

The first visual indication I had of the power of the explosion was not the Murrah Building, because it was shrouded in smoke from the burning cars. I could see that the roof of the Journal Record Building across the street was blown off and that the stone work on top was badly damaged. I knew it had to be big. I am a Vietnam veteran, and I had never heard an explosion so big or seen a single blast do that much damage. As I moved up the street, I could see that the entire front half of the building was gone all the way up to the roof.

∞

6

Downtown Oklahoma City.
— **Photo courtesy of David Allen**

Randy Britton is a lieutenant with the Lawton, Oklahoma, Fire Department.

As I got close to the front of the building, the hair stood up on my neck. I felt just like Richard Dreyfus in the movie *Jaws.* When he first saw the great shark come out of the water at the back of the boat, he simply said, "We need a bigger boat." That's what we needed in Oklahoma City that day, a bigger boat.

∞

Jerry Griffin was in the jury box in the County Courthouse hearing testimony in the third day of an assault and battery case at the time of the explosion.

I looked out to the north and saw a window washing platform, suspended by ropes on the west side of a tall building. It hung at a crazy angle, with the south side six feet higher than the north. Two or three people were trapped there. Any control they had over their environment had blown away.

I ran toward the building. I saw an elderly white woman carrying a black baby. A young black woman ran toward her screaming, "My baby! Is that my baby?" When she got within five feet of the child and saw its face, she turned west and continued running, screaming, "Where's my baby? Where's my baby?"

∞

Vernon Simpson is a major with the Oklahoma City Fire Department.

I was at the County Courthouse and headed on foot to

the Federal Building. I got there in minutes. It smelled like blood. A real strong blood smell, like at a bad car wreck.

We started digging, trying to get people out. If we heard somebody holler or saw something move, we tried to find them. At one point we saw blood dripping from the ceiling. We went up to that ledge and there was three of them laying up there — one alive and two dead.

∽

Sergeant Dan Helmuth was one of many police officers who were the first rescuers inside the building.

The police radio was going crazy. I pulled over at 4th and Harvey, crossed the street, and climbed the stairs to the plaza, heading toward the south entry doors. About twenty feet before I entered the building a lady came stumbling out, and as she passed me she took hold of my arm and said, "The day care is on the second floor. Make sure the children are okay!" I said I would, then entered the building, expecting to see walls, floors, and ceilings. I stopped dead in my tracks. There was no day care center, nor was there a second floor, or a third. Another police officer came running in and stopped beside me. "I know where the kids are," he said. "On the second floor."

"There's not a second floor," I informed him. The officer, whom I did not know, ran onto the pile in front of him and started digging frantically. It occurred to me that anything that had been on this level was probably below us now. I began to look for a stairway.

I found the stairs and went down to the basement. The metal door there had blown out onto the stairwell and I tried to move it. I was finally able to squeeze by it and climb over a big mound of building materials. I felt like I had walked into a dark cave. The air was heavy with insulation dust and the stink of concrete and burned flesh. Water pipes everywhere were leaking. Every time I moved I

9

bumped my head on dangling objects. Fighting an urge to just get out, I cautiously worked my way along the south wall to the pancaked area that later became known as the pit.

I saw what I thought was my first victim. He was dressed like a maintenance man. He did not appear to be injured and was standing very quietly staring at another victim. I yelled at him, "Hey, what are you doing down here?"

"I work here," he replied, not taking his eyes off the woman, who appeared to be gravely injured.

I asked him where he was when the bomb went off.

"Back there," he said, motioning over his shoulder to the parking garage.

The injured woman was lying on the floor about half-way back in the cave. She had a nasty looking wound behind her right ear and it looked like she was missing a piece of her skull. She was writhing and moaning loudly.

"She's hurt bad," I told the man. "We need to get her out of here." He did not reply and never looked away from her. Loose stuff started falling down around us and I grabbed him and pulled him back under a stairway. A moment later a large chunk of concrete dropped down from the upper floors and thudded at our feet. I hollered to the rescuers overhead to not kick or throw anything down.

I contemplated the idea of carrying the woman out by myself. Before I could decide, two EMTs appeared, picked her up, and carried her out. Other police officers were now coming into the area, including John Avera and a fireman. Two other trapped women had been calling out to me, begging to be rescued. One was getting hysterical because of the rising water. She was pinned under concrete and pleaded with me to get her out before she drowned. I assured her we would get her first, although I had no idea exactly where she was.

I worked my way around to the west side of the cave and found a pair of legs sticking out of the pulverized cement. I grabbed the right foot, hoping it belonged to one of the women crying out to us. There was no response to my touch and I knew immediately that this one was dead.

Sergeant Avera and the fireman were digging several

feet away when John suddenly exclaimed that he heard a baby crying. The three of us began to dig in a frenzy. John and the fireman then moved a piece of concrete and uncovered two small children. John picked up one of them, a small white girl later identified as Baylee Almon. The fireman picked up the second child, who turned out to be P. J. Allen, and handed him to me. I ran outside, handed the little boy to a deputy sheriff, then ran back into the basement and radioed Dispatch, advising that the electricity and water needed to be shut off quick. By now four or five fire rescue workers were in the area, so I made my way back upstairs for some fresh air.

As I was coming up the stairs the commander of the Marine recruiting office was telling some officers that he was still missing several people, including the young daughter of an employee. We went with him to the sixth floor to help him search. Sergeant Richard Armstrong came out of the Marine recruiting office carrying the child, a four or five-year-old girl. He struggled in the loose material, and I offered to take the girl, but he refused, so I grabbed him by the arm to help him across. He was followed by an injured Marine. I helped him across, too. Then Sergeants Rick Allen and Rick Dunn and I thoroughly searched that office, calling out for survivors. We searched the sixth through ninth floors in the same manner, but found no one.

Later, at the police command post, I saw that my uniform was a mess. My shirt was covered with blood and there was blood smeared on my left arm and hand. I was also covered with gray dust. As I walked the five blocks to my car that evening, the cold dismal rain we hoped wouldn't come had arrived.

∽

Russell Burkhalter is a corporal with the Oklahoma City Fire Department.

At 9:02 the door to the weight room flew open and I

11

heard a slight rumble. The ceiling tiles all lifted. I thought that someone had kicked the door open really hard as a prank. Next I heard the emergency buzzer ring twice. I figured someone was at the door ringing it. Moments later the lights kicked on and Dispatch started to call out rigs to assist with a Haz-Mat incident at 5th and Robinson.

Truck 5 was dispatched to go, so I hopped off the bike and went to the rig room. The rigs were gone! They had heard radio chatter and took off before being dispatched. I heard 620 tell Dispatch, "Send me every available ambulance." I knew it was something really bad even before I turned and saw the huge column of smoke rising over downtown. I grabbed my car keys and jumped behind the wheel. I knew 5th and Robinson was the address given, so I headed that way.

At 8th and Robinson I parked my car. I saw Truck 5 a block away, so I ran to the truck and hopped in. There was glass and debris all over the street and I was beginning to see the walking wounded emerge from everywhere. Lieutenant Ardery told me someone had set off a bomb in the Federal Building.

At the building's east side we hooked up with Captain Chris Fields and Corporal Steve Fitzgerald. I watched as police officers carried a badly injured black female from out of the basement area. She had shrapnel wounds from head to toe. Some of Engine 4's crew attended to her. Captain Fields told me to begin assessing and treating some of the other wounded that were being brought outside. Steve and Clint Greenwood, our driver, headed for the basement to look for more victims. I noticed a man carrying an injured child. He walked up to Chris and handed him the baby, which couldn't have been much over a year old. Later, the child was identified as Baylee Almon. Chris took the child and just cradled it in his arms.

∽

The Alfred P. Murrah Federal Building.
— **Photo courtesy of Oscar Johnson**

View of the Federal Building's southwest corner.
— **Photo courtesy of Penny Turpen James**

Police Sergeant John Avera's encounter with young Baylee Almon, though it lasted only a few seconds, was caught by a photographer and became a front-page image transmitted around the world.

I felt the concussion inside the room and saw the window bow in and out. I immediately started running in the direction of the smoke. At the site, a man approached me and told me there was a day care inside the building. I entered through a broken window and saw a uniformed officer removing a man from that room. Both were drenched in blood. I helped get them out the window, then looked around. Nothing was recognizable. Water was streaming down from the ceiling. Electric wires dangled everywhere. I noticed another officer behind me. We found two females in the dark and dusty room. We talked to them as we evaluated their injuries. One thought her leg was broken, and she hurt all over. The other one was in a lot of pain, also, but thought she was okay. We got them to the window, where people outside assisted them out.

We entered a hallway and walked east in the darkness. I could see the elevator shaft, its doors open. I heard some female voices calling for help. Officer Dan Helmuth and I started toward the voices; it was then we heard a baby crying. We dug like crazy into the pile of broken concrete trying to find that baby. One chunk was so big it took both of us to move it. Underneath we found not one, but two babies.

We each took one and headed for daylight. It was too dark to tell anything, but I knew my baby was badly hurt. Once we got outside I rushed toward the first fireman I saw and handed the child to him. I had no idea that a picture had been taken. I then returned to the ruins of the building to tend to the ladies near the elevator shaft. I found one victim, but the crevice she was trapped in was too small for her to get out. Eventually, more rescuers and equipment arrived, to include generator lights. I finally left when I felt I was mostly getting in the way.

I walked back to the police station, exhausted, and collapsed in a chair. I watched some news reports on television. I could not believe what they were saying.

∞

Chuck Porter's photos of a police officer and firefighter bringing one-year-old Baylee Almon out of the building were distributed worldwide following the bombing.

I work in a bank three blocks from the Murrah Building. I thought it was a sonic boom, and that some pilot was going to be in trouble for causing one this close to the city. Then some other employees saw the smoke, making me think an old building had just been demolished. I thought I'd grab my camera from the car, get a few good pictures, and only be gone about ten minutes.

About halfway to the car I saw the roiling black smoke from the burning cars, then I started seeing glass and twisted metal and injured people all over the place. I took my camera out and started snapping pictures.

When someone told me to move, I moved. I had been on the scene about ten minutes when the two photos so widely publicized were taken. The first showed police sergeant John Avera handing the baby to OCFD's Captain Chris Fields. The second was of Chris Fields holding the baby.

Downtown offices were evacuated about 10:30. I left and went to the Wal-Mart in Edmond and called Dan Smith, who is the director of photography at the University of Central Oklahoma, to ask him for some advice. Dan told me that, since I was down there so fast, I might have some images that would interest the media. He advised me to go to the Associated Press office with them.

When I picked up the developed photos, some of the Wal-Mart employees started asking about it. I handed them the pictures, and when they looked at them they all started crying. I drove to the AP office and asked them if they would like to look at some pictures I took of the bombing. They looked at them and said they would like to run the two.

The next thing I knew, they were published everywhere.

∞

Rick Allen is an Oklahoma City Police sergeant.

Broken drywall and insulation covered everything. Twisted metal and light fixtures drooped down from the ceiling. The dust was choking. I paired with Jeff Ramsey, and we crawled over and under debris looking for the lucky ones. For safety, we stayed within shouting distance of each other. At the time, we didn't have hard hats, masks, or even gloves. We weren't having any success finding anyone, so we went up another floor. I met an army serviceman there. He was bleeding from a cut on his forehead. He said he had been in the building at the time of the explosion and that several of his co-workers were missing from the floor.

I crawled my way across chest-high mounds of clutter, inching my way toward the northern portion of the fourth floor. I looked to the north from the blown-open building and saw the rest of the carnage. The roof was completely gone on a church across the street. A nearby parking lot had about thirty cars in it. Several were burning furiously among the torn and crushed ruins of others. I remember thinking to myself that President Clinton might have something to say about this.

∞

Officer Brad Lovelace is with the Oklahoma Capitol Patrol. He arrived on the scene almost immediately.

I met up with Officer Ben Blood and together we

started searching the Journal Record Building. After a while we were told that the building was unsafe and to get out. I headed for the Federal Building, and while crossing the street I was flagged down by two women. They asked, "Do you know where they are keeping the children?" I told them they were at the triage center by the YMCA. They asked me if they were okay, and I said they all looked okay to me, then I followed by saying, "You mean the kids from the YMCA day care, right?" They said, "No, the kids from the Federal Building day care." It was the first I knew of a child care center in the Murrah Building, and I can only imagine the look on my face as I said, "I don't know."

∞

Teresa Adams, a former EMT and police officer, runs an entertainment booking agency downtown. She was one of many citizens who provided first aid minutes after the bombing.

I couldn't drive all the way in, so I parked my car, grabbed my first aid kit from the trunk with both hands and ran the rest of the way. When I saw the building, an overwhelming rush hit me. I dropped my first aid kit and nearly fell to my knees. My heart pounded and I heard myself repeating over and over, "Oh, my God, Oh my God." I could hear my ears ringing and the air seemed thick and hard to breathe.

I picked up the first aid kit and ran across the parking lot to a grassy area where some people were gathering. Glass was still pelting the street from upper windows. Every building in sight looked like an abandoned shell filled with garbage. I started grabbing things out of the kit and so did several other people. Within minutes there was very little left.

As I handed out the few remaining bandages, a man came rushing by and placed a little girl down on the grass next to me. I assumed he had brought her out of the YMCA day care. She was covered with dirt and blood. It seemed like she would never stop crying "Mommy." I took her tiny hand and then hugged her gently. I told her several times I had already called her mommy and she would be here in just a minute. She finally responded. There were cuts on her face and head. When I started to pull away she held on tight. I told her I needed to go get more Band-Aids. "I'll be right back, I promise," I assured her. I looked for a place on her cheek where I could give her a kiss, carefully released her, then ran back to my car for more bandages as fast as I could go.

∞

Oklahoma City Police Sergeant Ronald Houck arrived at the Murrah Building moments after the blast.

At the time of the detonation I was at the scene of a stabbing at 5th and Dewey. The victim was being attended to by officers from the fire department and some ambulance attendants. I drove immediately to 5th and Hudson, figuring there had been a gas explosion. Bleeding people came out of nowhere. By the time the first ambulance arrived, I had over two dozen people standing near the corner of the intersection. A citizen asked if it was okay for him to transport wounded to a nearby hospital. He told me that he had a large van and could carry about a dozen passengers. Another person came up and said he had a truck that could carry eight. The truck and van pulled into the intersection and were filled with the less seriously injured.

Later, I saw a news video showing the van and truck arriving at St. Anthony Hospital.

∞

Larry Dellinger is a second lieutenant with the Oklahoma Highway Patrol.

I was on the fifth floor of the Oklahoma County Court-

18

The north side of the Murrah Building one hour after the explosion.
— **Photo courtesy of Penny Turpen James**

Wreckage left by the blast on 5th Street the morning of April 19.
— **Photo courtesy of Richard Hail**

19

house when the blast shook the building. I rushed to my patrol car and drove to the building's southwest corner. Paper and other clutter was still falling and drifting down. People started stumbling out of the south entrance. I advised Dispatch and asked for all available help.

One of the walking wounded asked me to go to the day care center on the second floor. I found a fireman and told him what she had said. He replied, "There is no second floor left." I entered what I thought was the second floor, but found only a crater.

I found a young woman with a broken ankle and helped her outside. She insisted she was all right and to go help someone else. I then found a badly injured lady trying to pull herself out of the smashed concrete. She had suffered massive cuts and appeared to be missing an eye. Even so, she too, insisted she was all right and told me to go help someone else.

I joined others at the day care site. We found parts of bodies. We found toys and baby shoes. I pulled a small pink sweater out and thought of the mother who had dressed that child that morning.

When I arrived home late in the evening I was exhausted and distraught. I've been a trooper for twenty-two years, but I was not prepared for what I'd just experienced. All I could think about was that small pink sweater. I tried to reason what kind of human being could do anything that vicious. But I could not.

∽

Sergeant Alan Prokop, a liaison officer for the Oklahoma City Police Department, was in his office in the nearby Municipal Court Building at the time of the detonation.

Officer Ron Bell was in my office at the time of the explosion, and together we jumped into my car and headed out. We arrived at the Murrah Building to find victims standing at the window openings on the third, fourth, and fifth floors, screaming for help. Another officer, named Washington, who was off duty, joined us, and as we approached the south entry an injured U.S. marshal was exiting the building. He told us that the explosion was a bomb and there were numerous victims trapped inside.

Officer Bell contacted Dispatch and asked them to get the utilities to the building shut off and requested that all available units, including Fire and Amcare, be sent to the scene immediately. About that time, someone coming out of the building said there was a day care center on the second floor and that as many as forty to sixty children might be trapped there.

We entered the building. The floors above the second floor entry had collapsed and the basement had also given way. Victims were buried under broken concrete slabs, bricks, and other building materials. The electricity was still on and many of the wires hanging loose were hot. Fires burned to the north of the building and the bodies of the dead and dying could be seen in the wreckage overhead and on some of the upper floors. The ceiling above had cracked under the weight of broken flooring, and as we checked the interior around us, large pieces of concrete continued crashing down from higher up.

Officer Washington found a victim trapped in a crevice, and immediately crawled down inside the tight opening. After a few minutes of struggling, he was able to lift her up and out to Ron Bell. While this was going on I attempted to support an unstable eight-by-ten-foot slab of concrete that was balanced directly over the victim. Once she was freed, Washington turned her over to me and I carried her from the building to the corner of 4th and Harvey, where several other victims were being cared for and awaiting transport.

I ran back inside and began assisting several of the walking injured. I then checked the area near the second floor's west end, where I found several toys. I spotted a man whom I thought was dead, so I carried him outside to the south plaza and left him with some medical people. As I re-entered the building the fire department was arriving on the scene. I discovered the body of a little black child, and made yet another trip to the plaza and the medical people. I went back to the same area, where two firefighters were also searching. Together we located three children who appeared to be alive. The firemen stayed inside to treat two of them, and the other one I carried out to an ambulance at 4th and Harvey. I then went back inside to try to find others. Detective Don Hull, whom I'd run into on the street, had followed me back in, and we each picked up one of the two remaining children the firemen had tended to. The limp little boy I carried out had suffered severe head injuries, but was still breathing.

I went back once again to assist the fire department. They had discovered a lady trapped in the basement area. I braced a broken six-inch pipe while they worked, and within a few minutes she was extracted and hustled outside for treatment. I climbed up over the second floor, where I found another victim, whom I carried out to the south patio. I then joined up with two detectives, Campbell and Burnett, who had been removing victims from the upper floors.

Sometime later the fire department ordered everyone out. About that time I observed detectives Campbell and Hill rescue two injured people from the shattered fifth floor. To allow the victims a safe avenue of escape, Campbell had to stand precariously on a six-inch ledge.

I had worked my way back down to the second floor when I found another victim near the elevator shaft. I carried her to the ambulance staging area about a block south, then we were once again ordered out of the building. This time we complied. Since I had a car at the site, I used it to transport police and fire personnel to the command center and Fire staging areas. Finally, I went back to my office, where I spoke with Major Heath. He observed the condition of my uniform and approved my leaving duty at about 2:00 P.M.

ॐ

***Don Hull is a detective sergeant with the
Oklahoma City Police Department. He was one
of the first rescuers on the scene.***

I arrived in a police car with Steve Carson and Jerry
Flowers, which we parked a block from the site. At 4th and
Harvey I was approached by a gentleman with a head injury.
He asked me for help. I looked at the left side of his scalp
and saw that he had a severe cut, and that a portion of his
scalp had lifted up away from his head. Using my hand, I
gently placed the gentleman's scalp back where it belonged.
I then took his hand, placed it there, and told him to keep
pressure on it until he could be taken to a hospital. I helped
him sit down on the curb to wait for medical help. I then ran
to the south entrance of the building, followed by Steve and
Jerry. I observed a man on the third floor sitting up and
calling for help at the edge of the building. Both of his legs
had been amputated at the knee and blood was pouring out.
There was nothing we could do. We had no ladder and no
other way to reach him. In a moment he fell back and was
silent.

The building's entrance was virtually blocked. Some police officers and citizens had already crawled their way in,
and we followed. I could hear the cries of children and
moaning from adults in the dim and dust-filled interior. Water was raining down on us, and pieces of concrete and other materials occasionally dropped from above.

We split up, and I ended up in the area that became
known as the pit, which was basically a large hole in the
ground that went down a couple of floors. Straight ahead
was a wall of broken concrete tablets stacked helter-skelter
for several stories. I moved west, and soon located a little
boy. He was removed and handed down a line of rescuers to
the outside. The next child was a little girl who had bright
red hair. She also was handed down the line to the outside.
Two more boys were found and they, too, were handed
down to the outside. We kept digging. After another three
feet or so, I found a small foot and leg. Others assisted, and

we managed to uncover the child. I thought he was dead, but when I moved his arm he gasped and started crying. He was bleeding profusely, so instead of passing him down the line, I cradled him and made my way outside, hoping there might still be time to save him. On three occasions between the building and the ambulance he stopped breathing. All three times I performed CPR and, like a little champ, he responded each time. I later found out that this little boy was Joseph Webber, twenty months old. He had fractured his jaw and palate, which restricted breathing. His eardrums were burst, and he had other injuries as well, but he survived.

I returned to the pit to keep digging and found myself in the company of a gentleman who looked like a construction worker. We dug and found a child who appeared to be four or five years old. The man said, "Oh, my God," and turned his face away when he saw the fatal head wound the child had suffered. I placed a hand on the man's back and told him that they needed his help outside more than inside. He asked if I was sure. I said I was a cop and he was not, therefore, he shouldn't be inside anyway. His eyes filled with tears and he quietly said, "Thanks." I never saw him again.

I took a blanket brought in for wrapping bodies and covered up yet another child. I carried this child out about the time the second bomb scare came. Just outside the entrance, I encountered Dr. Spengler, who pronounced the baby dead. A young nurse wrote the date, time, and the doctor's name on a piece of masking tape and stuck it to the child's stomach as I held him. She directed me to the courtyard, where benches had been covered with sheets and encircled with yellow caution tape. I entered the area and placed the child on a bench. I covered him with another sheet and knelt and prayed for him. I told him I was sorry I had to leave him there.

When we were allowed back inside, we began digging again. Over the next several hours I located four more dead children, all aged five or less, and three dead adult females, one of which was pregnant. I uncovered a small leg which ended just above the knee and the right hand of a child that

Harvey Avenue (northbound view) at the intersection with 5th
Street the day of the bombing.
— **Photo courtesy of Richard Hail**

View of the Athenian Restaurant building (left) and
the YMCA (right).
— **Photo courtesy of Penny Turpen James**

fit in the palm of my own hand. Other body parts were found throughout the day. Eventually, we were relieved by organized rescue crews. I was still in suit pants, tie, dress shoes, and bare hands.

You could smell the bomb. You could smell the death. Faces were blank. A priest walked up and asked if I was all right. I asked for some water. Sergeant Flowers took me back to the station, and I went to my office and sat at my desk. I couldn't talk to anyone. The other detectives in the office knew it was bad. My wife was contacted and came to pick me up and take me home. It was several days before I slept or ate again, and I knew it would be a lot longer before the wound in my own heart could even begin to heal.

∽

Jill Hull is the wife of Police Detective Don Hull.

I spent the morning worrying about my husband. He had worked in the Federal Building and often went there to visit friends. At approximately noon I saw my husband on television. He was holding what appeared to be a lifeless little boy. I could see he was telling a nurse or medic, "I can't, I can't."

Part of me felt relief. He was physically all right, but the frantic look on his face said he was much worse than the picture showed.

∽

Jerry Northcutt is a senior probation and parole officer with the Oklahoma Department of Corrections.

All available officers were asked to respond to the scene. We started seeing windows blown out as far away as 23rd Street. The destruction was worse the closer we got.

Thoughts of my friends at the District Attorney's Task Force flooded my mind.

When we got there, the first familiar face I saw was Vendell Underwood. He worked for DEA. I asked, "V, are you okay?" He replied, "No," and started crying. I put my arm around his shoulder and hugged him. We looked up at the ninth floor where his office had been. It was gone.

We began searching surrounding buildings, then the second bomb scare came. Afterward, I went into the Federal Building with a small group led by Officer Jerry Flowers. We climbed over rubble until we got to the area he said was the day care center, the one place we didn't want to be. Chunks of concrete and wires hung down everywhere. Dust and a strange smell filled the air.

We started digging. It seemed useless. The dust made it hard to breathe. Finally, I went outside for some air and a mask. I saw some officers I knew and asked them for a flashlight. I motioned for them to come with me and we moved out. Someone pointed up to the body of a man in a second floor window. He was blown against the wall but was looking out the window. I asked if anyone had tried to get him down. I was told they had tried earlier, when the man was still alive, but that he was pinned against the window and couldn't be moved. His leg was gone. They could do nothing but watch him die.

We went back inside to dig. It wasn't long before I heard a voice say, "I need a blanket." A dead child had been found. It was wrapped in a blanket and passed outside. It didn't seem real. After a few minutes, another voice said, "I need a blanket." This time I saw the child. It looked like debris had blown into his face. He was wrapped up and passed outside. Another voice, another child. I saw this child handed to Officer Gordon Nelson. I looked at his face —horror, sadness, pain. He held the baby for a moment and took him out. Another voice, another child. No one was alive.

I saw Officer Terry Rayner holding one of the dead children. The child's head and arm were missing. I looked at Rayner's face. Same horror, sadness, pain. I followed him

27

outside. I needed some air. I watched a rescue worker vomit when he saw the headless child. His buddy told him to keep on going. Officer Rayner handed the child to a nurse. I sat down for a minute, trying to find reality. I saw a photographer pull the blanket down from the headless child to take a picture. A nurse protested, but the photographer said it was for identification purposes. I then heard a voice say, "I hope his parents can identify him by his underwear." I thought to myself, "No way. We'll go find his head." Strange thought. Terry Rayner must have had the same strange thought.

We went back inside to look. We found his arm. No head. It was disappointing.

∞

Jack Willis, a parole officer with the Oklahoma Department of Corrections, was part of the early rescue effort.

We climbed a pile of rubble inside the building. A small child wrapped in a blue blanket was handed past me. Voices called for more blankets. I saw Officer Terry Rayner carrying a small bundle. Another officer asked, "You find one, Terry?"

He replied solemnly, "Only an arm."

∞

Joe Moore is an officer with the Oklahoma Capitol Patrol. He was less than a mile from the Murrah Building at 9:02 A.M.

When we arrived at 5th and Robinson, I asked an Oklahoma City police officer what he needed. He said, "Help the wounded to the triage area and move the police line back." We started helping the people that were hurt get to the triage area. All around them ordinary citizens that were uninjured started to help. We got the people and children that were in front of the YMCA moved to safety. An Oklahoma City police officer asked Ted McElreath and myself to move the crime scene tape line behind the YMCA. McElreath grabbed the tape and we started moving people back. As I did this, I passed the remains of the YMCA day care playground. Swing sets and slides were twisted and bent.

At the Federal Building, I climbed over, under, and through the piles of wallboard, ceiling tiles, file cabinets and I don't know what else, searching for anyone that might be in there. The first victim I found was a man. He was lying on his back. His left arm was tucked behind him, his left leg gone. Part of a fallen wall covered his upper body and head. It's strange; I could tell he was male by his clothes but I couldn't tell what race he was. I looked some more while thinking I was lucky not to have seen his face and eyes. I was on about the fifth or sixth floor when I found another victim. He was a black man lying face down and partly covered in rubble. He was also dead, and this time I did see his face and eyes. They were open and very blank. No expression.

The rest of the day is a blur. I don't remember driving home. I had a pop with me when I got home but I don't remember stopping to get it. When I got home I just sat and held on to my two sons and cried for about a half hour. My four-year-old son, Dalton, kept asking me what was wrong and why was I crying. I couldn't answer him. My wife, Teresa, told him simply that "Daddy has just seen a lot of people hurt and he is sad," as she rubbed my head.

Later that night a friend that was at the bomb site called to see if I was as messed up as he was. I was. He told me he got to help rescue a lady. I told him all I found was dead bodies.

∽

Francene Thomas is a police service technician for the City of Oklahoma City.

I was on my way to work downtown and was about to

make a left turn onto Lee from Sheridan when the bomb blew. A tremendous sound and then compression stabbed into my ears, and the shock wave shook my car. When my senses returned, I made the turn and pulled into the police department parking lot just as broadcasts started coming over the radio. I parked my car, got out, and ran to my city vehicle.

At Walker and 4th streets I fell in behind a fire truck and followed it east toward the scene. As I reached the intersection with Hudson I could see debris still falling and people running everywhere. Motorists were still trying to drive east, toward the building, so I pulled over at 4th and Robinson and started routing traffic out of the area. After a few minutes, I moved to another intersection, then parked again at 5th and Broadway and grabbed several pair of rubber gloves from my vehicle and headed in the direction of the YMCA. Dazed people were all over the place. I guided them to curbs for safety or for treatment to the first-aid areas already being set up.

From there, I continued on toward the Murrah Building. At the corner of 4th and Robinson, on the building's south side, I heard a man yell at me. He wanted help with a woman he was trying to restrain. She was screaming, "My baby's in there! Lord, have mercy, let me go!" I rushed over to help restrain her. I told her it was too dangerous inside and that we had to let trained rescuers do the searching. Finally I told her that if she would stay put I would go in and look for her child. She agreed, so I headed out.

I saw an off-duty officer I knew, named Chandler, coming down the steps. He was in street clothes and wearing one sandal. His other foot was bare. I said, "Chan, where's your shoes?" He said, "I was wearing sandals, but one got lost." I asked him if he was going back inside and he said he was. I turned, spotted a young man nearby, and asked him what size his shoes were. He said, "Eleven." I asked Chan the same question and he said, "Ten." I told the young man to give this police officer his shoes, and the man did so, without argument.

I asked Chandler if he needed help and he said, "Come

Unidentified casualties.
— Photo courtesy of
Richard Hail

The scene in the street in front of the Federal Building
on April 19.
— Photo courtesy of Penny Tupen James

on." Just as I turned to follow I saw the distraught woman again trying to get into the building, so I went back and calmed her once more. Meanwhile, Chandler disappeared inside. From where I stood on the plaza, the inside of the building looked as though it was filled with thick, gray fog. I saw officer Alan Prokop emerge from that fog and I asked him if they still needed help. He said "Yeah, do you think you can handle it in there?" I said I could and followed as he led the way over huge chunks of broken concrete, twisted steel, and tangles of wires.

Inside, I saw several men, some in business shirts, some in uniforms. All of them were digging with their bare hands, moving concrete and yelling, "I got another one over here. I need a sheet or something." The air was hard to breathe. Somebody asked me where my mask was. Nearby, someone else asked for a mask. I made my way outside to find masks, and quickly approached a lady with one of the medical teams with my request. While I waited, I heard a male voice behind me holler "Help!" and I turned to see a man holding a bundle in his arms and attempting to climb up over a huge, unstable concrete slab.

I ran over and extended my arms, then stepped down to take the bundle from him so he could make the climb. As he tried to hand it to me, I saw the exposed leg of a child. The leg had a large gaping gash in it that wasn't bleeding, and I realized the child was dead. I yelled "Wait," then climbed down the slab and got behind the man and braced him so he could make it up while still holding the bundle.

The woman returned with a box full of masks and I headed back inside. I encountered Sergeant Don Hull and he yelled that he had seen more bodies and for me to go get more body bags and sheets. Once again I climbed back to the entrance and told someone what I needed. I was told there were no more body bags and was handed a pile of sheets. A man nearby on the plaza approached, took off his sport coat, and said, "Here, take this." I went back inside and started handing out sheets every time somebody shouted for one.

The next thing I knew a second bomb scare forced

evacuation, so I bugged out with the others, then went from one block to the next, helping clear business owners from their offices in the vicinity. When the area was vacated, I just started walking west on Park Avenue, thinking it was just like a movie after the Martians have invaded — trash blowing down deserted streets, sirens wailing.

∽

Dr. Carl Spengler was the first physician on the scene. He had been having breakfast nearby with Heather Taylor, an EMT student.

We had just come off an all-night shift at University Hospital's Emergency Department. As a third year Emergency Medicine resident, I work entirely night shifts. Heather Taylor, myself, and another doctor were having breakfast at Cattlemen's restaurant. There was a loud concussion. I looked at the others and said, "That was an explosion." The other doctor, Jay, kind of shrugged it off. A minute later, a man backed through the restaurant door, looking skyward, and yelled something about the Federal Building.

I ran to the front door, turned left, and used the pay phone to call my house. My wife works only seven blocks from downtown. She answered, and I told her something bad had happened and not to go to work. I told Heather and Jay that I was headed toward the building. Jay was still skeptical, and said he would drop by the ER on his way home. Heather and I jumped in the car and off we went.

I ran every stop light racing toward the building. I weaved in and out of traffic, but could only get within three blocks of the Murrah Building before I was forced to park my car. Heather and I ran up the street. Other people had abandoned their cars. Still others, cut and crying, ran past us, heading the opposite direction. I had done a research paper on a disaster. Oddly enough, mine had been on a proposed terrorist attack on Oklahoma City. Ironically, the fictitious bomb I wrote about had exploded only three blocks from where the real terrorist attack had apparently just taken place. I realized this as we arrived at the site.

We saw one paramedic squatting on the ground, arranging equipment. There was a fireman there, too. Except for the paramedic, we all stood staring at the building for probably sixty seconds. There were desks, chairs, filing cabinets, and pieces of building still sliding off the exposed floors, falling haphazardly into a heap.

There was a man lying in the bomb crater next to us. I made my way down to him, only to discover he had been killed from either a fall or a crush injury. As I stood at the bottom of the crater, I could see a large slab of concrete where the dead man had hit after plummeting down. There was a large bloody splatter mark and a streaked trail where he had slid off the slab and rolled into the crater. I slowly turned, surveying my surroundings. Every building in the area had been laid to waste. I was awestruck.

I climbed out of the crater and saw two men lying just above the large slab of concrete. I climbed up the huge blocks to them. As I made my way, I lost my balance and fell over one of the men, who was lying on his back. We ended up almost face to face. He had been horribly crushed. The second man was partially buried face down. The pile was still shifting and settling, so I quickly reached up and grabbed him by the back of his head. When I lifted it, his face stayed in the broken cement. I simply dropped what I had in my hand and started down the pile. It was obvious that if I didn't get off the loose rubble I stood a fair chance of being buried myself.

A man staggered out of the southwest corner of the building and collapsed on the street. He had a severed carotid artery, and frothy blood bubbled out of his throat. The paramedic handed me some equipment and I attempted to entubate him (place a breathing tube through the mouth and into the lungs). My first attempt was unsuccessful, with me placing the tube down his esophagus. When I pulled the tube out, the poor man looked up at me and said, "Don't ever do that to me again." I apologized and, thankfully, the second try worked. We loaded him on a gurney and he was carried down the street to an ambulance.

A police officer I know, Steve Carson, came up and told me we were needed on the south side of the building. Heather and I quickly ran in that direction. When we got there, four paramedics were already hard at work. There were several people on the ground, some on back boards, and some lying on the sidewalk. I could not count the number of injured people sitting on the curb. The paramedics recognized me, and the five of us decided to make the southwest street corner the triage site. One of them handed Heather a bundle of triage tags and I instructed her to tag each patient with whatever diagnosis I yelled out.

As we moved through the wounded on the ground, no one cried or yelled for help. If the patient was conscious, they quietly waited for medical attention. Amazingly, some of the most critically injured patients were actually joking with me as I examined them. There was only one other person that I entubated, a woman. She had a crushed face, and what I thought was an amputated left foot.

Treatment was crude and swift. Some of my decisions were not popular with the untrained observers, but that's the nature of triage. Pressure bandages for the bleeding and spinal collars for everyone. No IVs, no resuscitations. We never saw a child come out alive.

∽

Dr. Don Chumley, an Oklahoma City osteopath, rushed to the scene from his office nearby, arriving on the Murrah Building's north side. As one of only two physicians on site in those first minutes, he helped remove victims and administer immediate first aid, all at great risk to his own safety. Tragically, Dr. Chumley died in a light plane crash near Amarillo, Texas, on

September 24, 1995, only five months after the bombing. His story is recounted here by a friend, T. D. Smith.

I turned on my TV and the first thing the news cameras showed was my friend Don Chumley tending the wounded. He was kneeling in a pit among the dead and dying, ministering to them frantically as their lifeblood drained away. Above him, nine stories of shattered flooring intermittently dropped boulder-sized chunks of concrete as they swayed and broke loose from skinny strands of rebar bent to the breaking point. One lethal slab missed his head by less than two feet, yet he never faltered. Nearby, an equally determined nurse was killed by just such a blow.

Only minutes before, the bomb had rattled the walls in his clinic at 18th and Broadway. He arrived at the site within minutes and immediately set up a triage area on the building's north side near the crater left in the street by the detonation.

In his reports, Don described the scene confronting him. "One man had his foot turned clear around. Both leg bones were broken. Three or four others had slashed jugular veins and were literally pumping blood out of their necks. One woman's jaw was exposed. As medical supplies ran out, I had to use Scotch tape to hold gauze bandages in place."

The number of lives he saved is unknown. What is known is that he treated seventy injured victims right there in the street before he was ordered to leave when a second bomb was thought to be found. Don left, but returned almost immediately. Back at the building, he was asked to enter the collapsed area that would become known as the "pit" to try and save several children and adults still trapped inside. He didn't hesitate, in spite of the pending threat. Following a U.S. Marshal into what turned out to be the ruins of the day care center, he remained there, helping extract victims, until late that afternoon.

We saw the carnage and the horror on television, hours of it. We also saw many examples of selfless heroism. The acts of individuals like Don Chumley enhance our own

Unidentified survivor awaiting rescue in the demolished Murrah Building.
— **Photo courtesy of Penny Turpen James**

A torn and punctured van stands in testament to the savagery of the blast.
— **Photo courtesy of Barbara Hernandez**

value by demonstrating that the human spirit can still transcend all fixed limits when faced with a life or death encounter, even when the life to be saved, at the risk of one's own, is a stranger. In a time when no one appears to care any more, this knowledge makes our world a more comfortable place. On that day, my friend Dr. Don Chumley was truly an American hero.

∞

Matthew Dunham is a volunteer disaster action team technician for the American Red Cross. He was on the scene by 9:30 A.M.

We arrived in the Emergency Response Vehicle about the same time as the firefighters. The streets and sidewalks were strewn with bricks, office furniture, stained glass, and wounded people.

"Who knows first aid?" someone shouted and we were off. I grabbed my lawn chair and supply stool and set up a triage area under a tree. A lady walking across the street asked, "Where's my baby?" She was wearing only one shoe and was bleeding from her right hand. I took her by the arm and sat her down on the curb so I could clean and bandage her wounds. I then treated a man with cuts all over his face and neck. "I was on the eighth floor," he said. "I'm not hurt. Treat someone else." After finishing him up, I set up another triage at the stairwell leading to the Federal Building's south patio.

I started treating others while a nearby EMSA crew cut away a man's clothes to get to his injuries. He yelled every time someone touched his wounds. He almost passed out from the pain when they lifted his head to wrap it with bandages.

With more experienced medics arriving by the minute, I got paired up with another volunteer. His name was Ed. We decided to go into the parking garage underneath the patio. As we walked in, we could hear men working in the darkness around the corner. As we got closer, I could hear the screams of the trapped victims.

∽

Ronnie Allen is a police officer with the Oklahoma City Police Department.

Large pieces of concrete dangled from twisted rebar. Children's toys and money from the Federal Employee's Credit Union were scattered in the ruins. Inside a collapsed north wall I found a woman completely covered by rubble except for her arm, which she moved from time to time.

∽

Reserve Deputy Scott Stephens is with the Cleveland County, Oklahoma, Sheriff's Department.

We formed a human chain to move backboards and other equipment down into a hole. We hoisted victims strapped to the boards back up and out. A firefighter down in the hole turned to shout something to another firefighter standing on the ledge when he saw a partially buried child just below the other man's feet. They freed her. She appeared unconscious. An EMT tried to take the child from the fireman as he carried her from the building, but the fireman said, "No, I got her."

The rescue workers in the hole were working to free a woman who had been covered up. Once she was out she was placed on a backboard and passed up. I remember she had a badly broken left leg. As we maneuvered out of the wreckage, the leg slid off the backboard. The woman was conscious, but beyond pain. I picked up her leg and placed it on the backboard. It was so shattered it felt like braided rags.

∽

Lynn Bourne is a captain with the Edmond, Oklahoma, Fire Department, eight miles north of downtown Oklahoma City. He arrived on the scene at 9:34 A.M.

The crew came into my office to find out what I had scheduled for the day, but before anyone had a chance to speak there was a thunderous boom. The entry doors flapped open and the whole building trembled. It made me want to crawl under my desk.

We all looked at each other and someone asked, "What the hell was that?" We ran outside and asked some roofers on top of the building next door what they could see. They said there was a cloud of black smoke in the downtown area.

We were immediately dispatched, and told to bring all our medical supplies, backboards, body bags, and Emergency Medical Technicians with us. We were asked to form a rope rescue team. Suddenly, I was somewhere else. It was twenty years earlier, and I was in Vietnam. It may have been the smell of death that triggered the time warp, or it could have been the screams or the bombed out buildings. Whatever it was, it had knocked me back right into the middle of the war. I felt helpless, with no place to hide. Then, just as suddenly, I snapped back to Oklahoma City again.

"Rope teams, let's go!" someone yelled. We searched the Journal Record Building from the basement to the top floor. The destruction was indescribable. It looked like someone had taken a tornado, thrown it inside the building, and shut the door. We found blood trails and swipes of flesh, but no bodies, alive or dead.

∽

Air Force Staff Sergeant Mark Scungio is from Covina, California. He has been stationed at Tinker Air Force Base for four years.

The city surrounding the blast site was quiet, almost

eerie. All the normal sounds of the city were gone: traffic, business, people. All I could hear was broken glass beneath my boots and helicopters overhead. Most of the sirens had been turned off. What was the point?

Two blackened firefighters ran past carrying an infant, a lifeless baby without an arm. I prayed for strength not to become sick.

Two men came up to me and said, "Here, take these and let's go!" It was hard trying to run and not fall amidst so many obstacles. I picked up two oxygen tanks and masks. When we got close to the building, so much dust and smoke filled the building that oxygen was thin. A "bucket-brigade" formed up and people passed chunks of rubble to each other, hand-to-hand. It was heavy, jagged stuff, and more than a little of it was wet with blood. The firefighters were so calm — Was this real?

The horror of it all gripped all of us again when cries for help came from the caved-in confines of the building. My faith was tested then, and the frustration of wanting to help and feeling helpless grew into determination to keep going, no matter what.

∽

Gordon Nelson is a senior probation and parole officer with the Oklahoma Department of Corrections.

It was like entering a cave. Duct work, pipes and electrical wires hung from everywhere. Voices of victims were occasionally heard making muffled cries for help. File cabinets were overturned and paper was everywhere. Somewhere I could hear a buried phone ringing. The phone continued to ring and ring. I pictured the caller desperately trying to determine if someone was okay.

∽

Stephen Davis is a corporal with the Oklahoma City Fire Department's Rescue Squad 16.

We entered the building from the south side. I found toys and a pair of baby shoes and realized with a sinking feeling that I must be in the area of the day care center. Images kept flashing into my mind of the way this place should have been — a room filled with laughter, children running, babies crying, teachers reading aloud with the kids in a circle around them. Instead, the place was a jumble of concrete and steel, everything splattered with blood. Making things even more difficult were the pictures of my own son's day care center which kept creeping into my mind.

Grisly encounters with the dead became almost routine as we continued with the rescue attempts. I was leaving the building as a result of another reported bomb, when I was confronted with a well-dressed woman, still sitting at her desk and pinned to her chair by a slab of heavy concrete. She could have been my wife, my mother. Somewhere, there was a family waiting to hear from her.

∽

Barbara McEndree teaches at the University of Oklahoma College of Nursing.

Broken glass, broken buildings. Venetian blinds fluttered from broken windows. People were just doing their jobs. For me, this was the twilight zone. I shivered.

We set up in a parking lot at 5th and Broadway in groups of four. Each group had a parking space. A couple walking by gave us their personal bedspread to sit on. Ambulance after ambulance brought us supplies. They would ask what we needed to stabilize patients, then they would return with more supplies. We had created an outdoor hospital. A nursing student caught up in the chaos asked, "What is triage?" I responded factually, but swallowed with horror.

This was the end of innocence.

Inside the YMCA day care center soon after the explosion.
— **Photo courtesy of Barbara Hernandez**

Mangled cars smolder in the 5th Street parking lot opposite the
Federal Building.
— **Photo courtesy of Penny Turpen James**

Randy Rognas works in the circulation department at **The Daily Oklahoman.**

Although I had every opportunity to take pictures of injuries, I took very few. One man in a shirt and tie was holding a girl of about five or six in his arms walking back and forth trying to comfort her while she was bleeding from her right eye and face. Instead of taking the picture that the professional would and learning their identities, I offered to take them to the hospital. His reply stunned me when he said, "I don't even know her. Her mother is in there somewhere."

∞

Scott Wilson is an officer with the Oklahoma Capitol Patrol.

I heard Brad Lovelace on the radio saying, "I've got people down everywhere. Send everyone we've got to help." I was driving north on Lincoln when I heard Don Hennessy ask for a unit to transport him downtown. I knew that Don was an EMT, so I went and picked him up.

We finally got through to 5th and Broadway. I remember seeing officers Ted McElreath and Ben Blood at 5th and Robinson. I went over and we started asking each other "Why?" About this time a frantic woman tried to break through the police tape that had been put up. Ted and I went over and told her we couldn't let her through and she said, "My child is in the day care center!" We told her again that we couldn't let her through and she said, "You don't understand. My baby is in there!"

We directed her to the command post and gave them her child's name to see if she had been rescued. Later, when I was watching the news, I saw a woman who was talking about her child who had been killed in the explosion. I then realized who she was. It was the same woman. It was Baylee Almon's mother. I was really shaken up about that.

∞

Sheryl Mapes is the program director for the American Lung Association of Oklahoma. She relates here an encounter with death by Registered Respiratory Therapist Laurie Ashford.

At the instant the bomb went off, Laurie Ashford was driving past the YMCA building in downtown Oklahoma City. Directly across the street, the Murrah Building's entire north side had been ripped off.

Laurie's van was thrown violently against the side of a parked car. Dazed, she looked out her driver's side window and saw the body of a badly burned victim crushed between her van and the car. She then heard someone calling her for help. It was a police officer carrying two small children from the YMCA day care center. Both children were lacerated and bleeding. She put them in her van and, after the policeman assured her there was nothing she could do for the crushed individual next to her, she started for the nearest hospital. Within a block, she was approached by several people desperate for medical help. She put as many as she could in her van, then raced five blocks to St. Anthony Hospital.

Before the day was out she made five more trips downtown to pick up wounded and deliver them to four different area hospitals. It was a day that changed her life forever.

∽

Corporal Ricky Harris is assigned to Station 1 of the Oklahoma City Fire Department.

I was peeling potatoes when I heard the boom. I thought an airplane had crashed. When we got to the scene I grabbed some medical supplies and started toward 5th Street. People were literally running toward me, all of them hurt. We decided to direct all the injured people to 6th Street, where a first aid station had been quickly set up.

Lieutenant Rick Yarbrough and I worked our way to

the front of the Water Resources Board Building, where a man told us there were people trapped on the third floor. We helped remove one severely injured man, then moved next door to search the adjacent building. That's when the report of another bomb came in. I looked out from the second story and saw people running everywhere. We started running, too, but could not find a way out, so we jumped to the first floor, then jumped out a window and ran to 6th Street.

Later, we continued the search, staying on until about midnight. I was then assigned to the command post, where I helped direct personnel to the site until 4:30 A.M. I was exhausted, but I would've stayed indefinitely if they would have allowed it. The situation was desperate.

cn

John Cresswell was the A. P. Murrah Building Manager.

It was my building. At a few minutes till 9:00 I went across the street to the courthouse to take my break. At first I thought the explosion was in the courthouse. When I saw the smoke I was shocked. I remember thinking, "It's my building." I made it outside and ran across 4th Street. My one thought was to get to the day care center. I saw little PJ's grandmother. A couple of guys were holding her back.

I headed for my office area, but the door was jammed and wouldn't budge. I went through another door, and when I got to where the day care was supposed to be, it wasn't there. A firefighter coming through asked me if I knew the building very well. I told him that it was my building. I knew every cubby-hole and corner. He told me to report to the Fire Chief. When I did, the Fire Chief told me to stay with him, that he was going to need to know things about the building.

I was trying hard not to think that this might be my fault. I was sure that a gas line or the boiler had blown up and caused all this destruction. I spent the rest of the day mulling that over. For some reason I just kept thinking that the whole thing might somehow have been my fault. After all, it was my building.

$$\infty$$

Jimmy Ferguson was in charge of mechanical operations and maintenance at the Federal Building. He was in the courthouse breakroom with John Cresswell. Once across the street, they went separate directions.

I found a lady who was totally covered with trash. She could hardly breathe. I pulled stuff from her face so she could breathe, then I found a second lady nearby. I cleared off the junk on her face so she, too, could breathe better, then went back to pull the first lady out. She had been blown on top of a pile and then covered by some other junk from the ceiling and walls. She was lying at an odd angle and I could tell she was really hurt. A couple of people showed up with a litter and asked if I needed it. The three of us finished freeing her and got her on the litter. They took her away. I never knew if she made it or not.

$$\infty$$

Oklahoma City Police Sergeant David Riggs helped with the initial rescue effort.

As we were pulling a file cabinet off a trapped woman, I saw a small child being carried out. The baby was wrapped in a blue blanket. All I could see was the left leg from the knee down and a small white hi-top tennis shoe on the foot. At that point my mind raced back to April 17, when my wife Cheryl and I took our granddaughter Taylor to the mall and bought her a pair of white hi-top tennis shoes. As I went back to work I pushed the tears back. A giant knot began to grow in my stomach.

∞

Mike Mahoney is a captain with the Oklahoma City Fire Department.

I was on the phone with my girlfriend. Even though I was sixty-six blocks south of downtown, it sounded like a sonic boom. I hung up, turned on my fire department scanner, and heard Chief Marrs reporting damage to several buildings downtown. I grabbed my jacket and ran out the door.

I reported to the command post and helped get things set up. While running a message to another officer, I got my first look at the building. Remaining walls looked like they had been sprayed with gunfire. Cars everywhere were twisted and burned. The front of the building was a smoking pile of cement, steel, and glass. I was asked by some medical technicians for some help, so I followed them across the street to a parking lot which was littered with chunks of concrete and the hulks of burned out cars. Behind one of the cars, the body of a woman lay covered by a blue plastic sheet. We rolled her into the sheet and carried her to the makeshift morgue. She wasn't the first there, but she was the first for me.

As I walked back across the street to find the officer and deliver my message, I kept thinking, "A man did this! It wasn't a tornado or some other natural disaster. It wasn't an accident. A man did this. He did this on purpose."

∞

Architect James Loftis was on the Murrah Building's design team. He was at the scene within ninety minutes of the explosion.

Southbound view on Harvey Avenue from the intersection at
5th Street.
— Photo courtesy of Penny Turpen James

Fallen street sign.
— Photo courtesy of Penny Turpen James

After attempting to help at Presbyterian Hospital, it dawned on me that the emergency workers probably didn't know the organization of the building. I could help them figure out how to get in and out, and there might be some questions I could answer. So, I got in my car, drove downtown, and approached a fireman at 8th and Harvey. He took me to the Chief. The Chief said, "Let's get this guy down to the site with some plans."

They got me some plans for the building, put me in a little van, and took me down to 5th Street, where I sat out in front with all these firefighters. I did a real quick orientation with the fire department's safety officer on both sides of the building, then filled them in on the layout, the circulation, how you get in here, go there, and so forth.

The bomb took out three of the main columns supporting forty-foot spans across the north side of the building, then took out one column in the interior span. Two others were badly damaged, but held.

∞

Oklahoma City Police Sergeant Linda Bray was two blocks from the building, investigating a minor stabbing when the bomb went off.

I was assisting on a stabbing call at 600 N. Dewey. I was standing just inside, interviewing witnesses when there was a great force that blew both doors inward and then knocked me backwards across the room. We all thought the stabbing suspect had hidden in the upstairs and had tried to blow up the building.

Everyone then ran out to the intersection of NW 5th and Dewey. I set up a roadblock there as people came running from everywhere. We helped injured people by finding willing drivers of private cars to drive wounded to nearby hospitals. I remained at this roadblock all day, directing emergency personnel to their appropriate command posts and assisting people in trying to obtain the whereabouts of their families.

The stabbing suspect was so shaken by the bombing that he went to the police station to turn himself in. He was advised to come back the next day, which he did.

cσↄ

Roy Widmann is assistant fire chief for the Mustang, Oklahoma, Fire Department. He is also a staff hydrologist for Kerr-McGee Corporation. On the morning of April 19, he was at his desk on the twentieth floor of the Kerr-McGee building in downtown Oklahoma City.

When I heard the blast I dove to the floor. Thirty seconds later I got up, looked outside. Smoke was filling the sky. Falling glass rained past my window from higher up. When the shock wore off, I ran to the other offices, checking for injuries, then got on the phone with my fire department. A co-worker, Jami Poor, had run up the street to check on the damage. Just as I hung up, she came back with her arms full of caution tape and latex surgical gloves. "They need these down there," she said, then turned back toward the elevator. We put on hard hats and headed for the street. We made our way to the triage center on the east side of the Federal Building and began helping out. I soon lost all track of time.

The report of another bomb came just as there was a lull in triage activity, so I took off running with everybody else. I ran about a block and a half and hunkered down behind a concrete retaining wall. One of the ATF agents there said we should take off our glasses in case of a blast. I looked up and saw that we were directly under a number of power lines. "Great!" I thought. "When the bomb goes off, if I'm not killed by the blast, I'll be electrocuted." I expressed that concern to the others, and we all took off running to the east.

51

We were stopped by a slow moving train at a crossing about a block away. It was going about one mile an hour, and it was pulling chemical tank cars. "Swell," I thought again. "We're worried about another bomb, and we're taking refuge next to a train loaded with chemicals."

We moved on once more, this time to an automobile repair shop. There, after I caught my breath, I pulled myself together and decided to return to my office. At this stage, with organized crews at the site, there wasn't much more I could do anyway, except stay out of the way. I figured my office might be the safest place to do that.

cm

Marc Woodard is a major with the Oklahoma City Fire Department.

If it hadn't been for a bowl of noodles, we would have been right down there at 5th and Harvey when the bomb exploded. We were scheduled for a training exercise but were delayed by one of the guys, determined to finish a bowl of noodles. We were still in the station when it happened.

When we arrived at 5th and Hudson, we were bombarded by wounded, fifty or sixty of them. Anybody who could walk or crawl, we directed to the Regency Tower apartment building at 5th and Hudson. There was so much happening at once, it was tough deciding what to do first. We started putting out car fires and sent a crew to the Water Resources Board Building. Later, at the Federal Building, another bomb scare forced evacuation. As I was leaving, I ran into a firefighter from another crew. I told him to leave, but he had found a woman still alive and didn't want to leave her. He said that he had uncovered her arms, and was about ten minutes away from getting her out. "Listen," I said. "We gotta get out of here."

"Major, I'm too close," he argued. "I have to stay and dig her out."

"We can't," I replied, "we were told to leave."

He just stood there staring at me. He wasn't budging. I tried to think of some convincing piece of logic that would persuade him to move.

"Listen," I said again. "What about your wife and little girl? You can't do them or this woman any good if you're dead. Am I right?"

That seemed to get through. He turned to me and said, "Promise me I'll get to come back and finish the job."

I told him I would see what I could do. He didn't get to come back, though. Someone else finished the job. Later, he went to the hospital to visit her and take her some flowers.

∞

Craig Bishop is a volunteer firefighter and disaster action team captain for the Cleveland County Chapter of the American Red Cross. He was on the scene minutes after the blast.

During the mayhem, I used a multi-plier pocket tool to free a woman from a telephone and computer cable. Myself and another unknown civilian rescuer started out of the wrecked building with her.

"Out! Everybody out!" we heard someone shout. My unknown fellow rescuer and I looked in each other's eyes. No words were needed, we each knew what the other was thinking — we can't leave her, we're too close.

We didn't know why everybody was being ordered out. About the same moment we heard, "Everybody out, there's another device," her body, once tense with pain, went limp.

Again, no words, just eye contact. We gently laid her down. I checked for vital signs and then stepped back. My partner did the same.

"Out! Everybody out!"

I knelt to continue as my partner put his hand on my shoulder. He said, "She's gone. We'd better go."

∞

Oklahoma City fireman Clinton Greenwood of Station 5 spent all day at the bomb site on April 19.

We rushed toward downtown not really knowing what we had. I was driving Truck 5. At 13th and Hudson, the Oldsmobile dealership looked like it didn't have a window left. We maneuvered west on 10th Street to Robinson. People were lying in the street. Cries of pain mixed with sirens made an already tense scene even more so. We stopped at 6th and Robinson next to the Southwestern Bell Building. Glass from above was still showering down on people below.

Eventually we made our way to the Murrah Building and entered the collapsing basement. The blast had ruptured water mains and it was already almost knee-high. Every once in a while the crackle of electricity, followed by sparks, would illuminate the area, which was dark. Dark like a cave. Others were there, working frantically to find survivors. A lady was found alive. We decided to just scoop her up and run with her on a back board.

Back outside, a district chief assigned me to recon the front of the building to see if we could ladder it on the north side. I jogged down the front of the building, passing the husks of burned cars. There were only spots to place maybe two ladder trucks. I relayed that information and it was decided that the northeast side was our best bet. Trucks 7 and 8 were also preparing to ladder the building in the middle and northwest locations.

Olen Ardery, driving Truck 5, attempted to back it into place, but couldn't get close enough to be effective because of the rock piles strung all along the street. This situation quickly changed, though, as several civilians, police officers and sheriff's people nearby quickly cleared a path. Above, marooned survivors waited nervously. Bart Everett went up first. Then I took a turn, followed by Mark Mollman.

Only minutes after we got them down, everyone began running and yelling from the building. We were still stand-

Fire department ladder trucks in action immediately after the explosion.
— **Photo courtesy of Penny Turpen James**

Rescuers remove a victim's body during early search and rescue efforts.
— **Photo courtesy of Penny Turpen James**

ing on top of the cab of Truck 5. I turned and looked. The rookie firefighters that had just been brought down were in a dead sprint away from the building. This wasn't a good sign for us. We leaped from the top of the cab to escape, then sounded the air horn to signal people inside to get out. They ran from the building in waves, screaming about another bomb.

We regrouped at 8th and Harvey. After the bomb scare, we organized a task force and entered what became known as "The Pit" and the daycare area. We found quite a few victims. Too many. Emotions were running high. Several hours later we came out for a break and were astonished to see who had showed up. Some of the first Urban Search and Rescue Teams (USAR) had arrived from Phoenix. Search dogs were on site, as well as several large cranes. Fire stations from around the state had come in to the city to cover our stations.

Tired, dirty and still disbelieving, we gathered our equipment and returned to the station. I felt different. I had done the best I could but still felt like we had lost. Most of the crew's families had come to the station, worried about their husbands and dads. This was something I needed desperately. I really needed to see my three boys and my wife.

For the men of Station 5, that night was the first in a series of sleepless nights.

∽

Scott Young is chief technologist at the VA Medical Center's Department of Nuclear Medicine.

A disaster alert sounded at the VA. Hundreds of VA employees scrambled to stations around the medical center. I felt I could best help in the ER. There I teamed up with our Assistant Chief of Staff, Dr. Steve Orwig, an RN named David, and a PA student for OU. We went downstairs to the ambulance entrance and waited.

A VA van pulled up. Kevin, the driver, said, "I'm ready to roll!" The four of us climbed in. Kevin got us downtown within minutes. When we got close we hit the roadblocks. Kevin shouted to the officers, "I've got a team of doctors from the VA. They're gonna help!" We were sent through immediately.

When Kevin got us as close to the bomb site as he could, we got out and headed toward the Murrah Building. Once we arrived at the northeast corner of the building, we triaged a few patients with lacerations and contusions, then waited for more. I surveyed the blast zone to the north. I still could not believe my eyes. I felt my face getting tight and my eyes burning. I had to stay strong on the outside, but on the inside I was a screaming, crying victim.

Policemen, firemen, and FBI agents were all over the place. A few minutes later a large detective-type guy began shouting, "FBI, FBI. Get up here!"

Within minutes a cry rang out, "Clear the area! Another device has been found!"

As the cry was repeated I looked to the east end of the building. All I could see was a wall of firemen, policemen, ATF agents, and FBI men running directly at me. We ran too, hurdling fire hoses, glass, and first aid supplies.

I don't know how far we ran, but it was several blocks. After catching our breath, we felt we could be of more help in the ER than standing around waiting for the all-clear, so reluctantly, we headed back to the VA.

∽

David Hackett is the disaster coordinator for the American Red Cross.

It was about 10:30 A.M. when the other bomb scares started. It became frustrating — we would start to get set up and organized, and then we would have to run up the road. The third time we had to do this I was so mad with the situation I just walked. People were running to safety, but some, including myself, just walked. I was tired and upset that we couldn't do our job and help.

∽

Ron DeVean is an EMT employed by EMSA.

I was trying to enter the building when people gathered out front began running away. Firefighters came out of the building, falling down from running so hard. I thought the building was about to fall. Then I heard people yelling that there was another bomb. I started running too.

Later, when I entered the building, two firefighters said they heard a female voice. To reach the victim, we set up a human chain, and for thirty or forty minutes we passed rocks weighing more than fifty pounds. Large slabs of concrete had been stacked up over us like cards. Each time a piece was moved, small chunks and dust fell on us and we would stop for a second, until the suspense passed, then we'd continue digging.

When we reached the victim, she was almost totally buried. She had no pulse. I wiped off her face, said I was sorry, and said a prayer. Before she died, she told the firefighters that there was another trapped woman, still alive.

Thirty minutes later we found her. We were able to slide her out through a small opening in the rock pile and put her onto a spineboard. Her vitals were stable. She said she didn't know where her arm was. It was intact, but was crushed. I told her I was a medic and that she was going home. She looked at me, tried to smile, and reached up to squeeze my arm.

At the hospital, family members crowded the lobby, looking at lists. They had brought pictures of their loved ones. I was called to the phone many times, but one call brought the entire horror of it into focus. It was from Children's Hospital. A family there was looking for a little girl, a one-year-old with brown hair and wearing a yellow playsuit. I told them to call the morgue because earlier in

58

the day I had sent a bundled baby up there. I soon realized we were talking about the same baby.

∞

Tony Lippe is an Oklahoma County Jail nurse.

As I ran toward the Federal Building with Lynn and Debbie, I saw one of our night shift nurses coming out of a heavily damaged high-rise apartment building. We checked her, and she was all right. Next, we came upon an injured postal worker. Debbie started working on him while Lynn and I continued to the north side of the Murrah Building with our box of supplies. We started working with some paramedics to set up a triage area. They told us to set up our stuff on the south side instead. I remember grabbing about 15 IV bags with tubing and running to the other side. The south side of the building was like a patio area that was now being used for triage.

Now we were all separated from each other and I entered the building on the south side. There was glass everywhere. I was crawling under some fallen rubble when I started seeing children's toys all over the area. I had crawled over several bodies, which were not all intact, when I saw a little blond headed boy lying on his side with his head tucked under his body. I don't remember seeing any physical injuries. He looked peaceful. I continued to crawl toward him in a very tight space. Just before I reached him, he let out a wheeze. I started CPR, but it was futile. The only light I had was a small pen light I was holding in my mouth. I just sat there and held him in my arms. Someone had brought in several blankets, so I wrapped him in one and continued to hold him.

The next thing I knew, people were leaving the building as fast as they could, but I just kept on holding this little boy. Somebody was shouting, "There's another bomb. Get out!" I didn't move. All of a sudden, an Oklahoma Highway Patrolman grabbed me, pulled me to my feet and ushered me toward the south patio area. I was still holding the little wrapped boy. As we exited the building, the patrolman let me go. I laid the little boy on what I think was a park bench.

ω

Sergeant Robert Campbell is one of many Oklahoma City Police officers who were on the scene within minutes of the detonation.

Sergeant Nick Pittman and I arrived on the east side of the building and ran to help a maintenance man who was dragging a long ladder across the top of the first floor. We climbed up and joined several other people in helping him raise the ladder toward the third floor. We set the ladder up on a large piece of broken concrete and, while Nick held it steady, another officer, known to me only as Eric, started up the ladder, followed by myself and a fireman. We climbed toward a large sloped window sill that would give us access into the building.

As we entered the third floor we were confronted by several people. All of them were very bloody. We tried to figure out who was hurt the worst, then started taking them down in order of need, as best as we could tell. The fireman took the first one, then was called off to go help somewhere else. After covering the broken glass on the window sill with a torn curtain, Eric and I worked it out whereby he would go up and down the ladder while I stayed topside, searching the floor for others and preparing injured victims to go down.

Each time Eric got to the top of the ladder, I positioned another victim right at the edge of the window sill, then lowered them to the point where Eric could reach their feet and guide them onto the ladder. Blood covered everything, even the rungs of the ladder. Blood also dripped down on me from a crack in the floor above. We lowered five victims down to other officers on the first floor. Farther below, I could see rescuers on the ground removing children and

The heavily damaged Journal Record Building at the corner of
6th and Robinson.
— **Photo courtesy of Jack West**

Ambulances stand ready at the corner of 5th Street and Harvey.
— **Photo courtesy of Penny Turpen James**

61

bodies from the building. After a while, Eric came back topside and helped me search for more victims.

As we continued looking, we found a number of bodies and body parts, but no more survivors. We raised another ladder to try and reach the fourth floor, but couldn't, so we returned to the exposed first floor and moved our ladder into another area that led back into the building. Inside, I could hear people yelling and crying.

I crawled into a space that had been a window with three others and together we moved toward the voices. We discovered two survivors and were able to get them out the back side of the building. From there, I worked my way into a stairwell and immediately heard trapped people shouting from somewhere up above. A few of us headed up the stairs, taking time at each level to look for victims. Myself and someone I knew only as Chris made it all the way to the ninth floor, where we found some federal agents digging frantically through the debris in search of a fellow agent.

Suddenly I heard a lot of yelling outside. I looked out a window and all I could see were people running away. I thought that either the building was breaking up or another bomb had been found. We ran for the stairwell, hoping to get out before the walls came down.

Once outside, I joined officers Rod Hill and Jim Ramsey, who were looking up toward the top floors. They were looking at two women still trapped there. Even though we had been ordered out because of the bomb threat, Rod Hill ran back inside. A minute later, Ramsey and I decided to go in, too. On the way up we were forced to crawl and climb over several obstacles. Rod had located the women near the southeast corner of the seventh floor, right where a large section of the floor had been blown away, preventing their escape. Rod found a very narrow edge of concrete still protruding from the south wall where the floor had once connected, and decided to try it. He sucked up against the wall, then without hesitation scampered across the ten-foot long gap. As he moved along, the edge crumbled and stuff literally fell out from beneath his feet. To reach the ladies, he then had to climb along a blown-out window, as the remaining floor was buried in debris and just too unstable. When Ramsey and I got to the drop-off, I started across, too. I made it okay, then looked for something to use as a bridge. I found a long piece of flat metal and laid it across the ledge to help support our weight.

Rod brought the first lady up onto the window frame, then delivered her to me. I advised her to keep her feet on the metal plank and to stay against the wall. I then told her to use her right hand to grip my shirt and to slide her left hand down the wall. Once set, we slowly made our way to solid flooring. When we got close, Ramsey reached out and grabbed us. Rod was waiting with the second lady when I got back, and we repeated the process. As soon as we were safe, the whole bunch of us exited the building as fast as we could go.

∽

Police Sergeant Rod Hill entered the building during the second bomb scare to rescue two women trapped on the seventh floor.

I had been helping tape off an area on the south side with perimeter tape when I noticed two women on the seventh floor standing by the windows. At the time, I thought those ladies should not be up there rummaging through the building. I guess my brain wasn't working very clear. About that time everyone started yelling about another bomb, and we were ordered to clear a four-block radius. It was then I realized those ladies were trapped where they stood. I thought they might jump when they saw everybody scattering. One of them yelled "Don't leave us!" So instead of running off with everybody else, I headed into the building and started up the stairs. Halfway up I encountered an ATF agent coming down the stairs. He was bleeding, but told me he could make it down on his own, so I continued on until I spotted the filing cabinet I knew the women had been standing near.

I hollered for them to stay calm. After catching my

breath, I started figuring a way to get them out. I decided the safest way to reach them was through the blown out reception window in what had once been their office. I worked my way toward them, stepping lightly. I touched a table top for balance and it collapsed to the floor. Most of the floor was missing. I had no way of knowing how stable it was, either, so I stayed as close to the outside wall as possible. It still looked too dangerous, so I stepped outside onto the window ledge, which was about 18-24 inches wide. It was scary, but it looked safer than the fractured floor. When I reached the two ladies, I explained that we would have to walk on the window frames.

When I was sure they understood the plan, I got back out on the ledge. The first lady squeezed between the file cabinet and the window frame, then got up on the frame itself. She held onto my neck, and we inched our way to the other side of the blasted out floor. It was about that time when I heard the voices of Detective Robert Campbell and Officer Jim Ramsey from the bike patrol. I gave the first lady to Robert and went back for the second one. I got her up on the window and repeated the process. When we reached Robert and Jim, we all headed down the stairs and got out of the building. I did not see the ladies again and did not even know their names.

On the following Tuesday, the two ladies were on *Nightline.* The next day, Channel 5 called me and scheduled a time for me to meet them. On Sunday, April 30, I was reintroduced to the two ladies from the seventh floor — Rhonda Griffin and Glenda Riley.

∞

Dentist Kathy DeHart abandoned her Oklahoma City office to provide on-site assistance.

I called Lydia, my best friend and an LPN. "Are you going?" I asked. "I'm getting dressed as we speak," she answered. We agreed on a meeting place downtown. Once there, we joined a group of volunteers. Doctors were asked to come to the front. A man with a camera walked up to me and said, "I'm from the medical examiner's office and I need someone to witness as I take pictures of the dead for identification purposes." We went over to the bodies lying next to the south patio area. One by one, I unwrapped the bodies of five children.

Their wounds were extensive. The first child was a little black boy. He had a red shirt and blue jeans and tennis shoes. He was covered with a fine white silt. Later, I learned the children would have been eating breakfast. I imagined them sitting at the table. The table must have provided some kind of shield for their lower bodies.

We proceeded. One blanket held two children. Lydia helped me untangle the blanket. We couldn't tell if they were boys or girls. They were both white. One was decapitated. There was a doll head wrapped up with this child. The medical examiner asked me to place the doll head close to the body. He thought it might help with identification.

cos

Michael Loruse is a sergeant with the Oklahoma City Police Department.

My wife was screaming, "Moose! Moose! Wake up! There's been an explosion downtown!" I headed to the scene, parking at 8th and Hudson streets. When I arrived at the patio area on the south side of the building, I discovered about fifteen officers on the scene trying to determine the facts surrounding the second bomb scare. I went inside with others to look for more children.

We started digging with our bare hands. We found dolls, diaper bags and parts of cribs. An officer next to me discovered a dead child. As he was dug out, someone said we needed to cover him in case his parents were outside. I took off my blue flannel shirt in order to wrap the child up. Others were recovered. A rescue worker came over with a stack of disaster blankets for wrapping the bodies. I used one on the baby I had, then cradled him in my arms and made my way to the south patio. I then went back and resumed digging.

I saw a wide range of emotions. One officer became physically ill when the second child was discovered. Another had tears in his eyes. One walked around carrying a doll head. He walked up to me and angrily handed it to me. He said, "Take it! Take it! I can't look at it anymore. Get rid of it." He handed me the doll head and began to dig again. I looked at the little doll head in my hand and thought that, in a way, it represented all the children in the building. I looked at another officer and we both stared at each other, wondering how this officer was being affected by this horrible scene. I took the doll head and casually tossed it aside. The officer that had carried out one mutilated child walked over to me with a stunned look on his face and said, "The child that I carried didn't have a head." I told him, "Yes, I know. This is the evil that men do."

We started digging again.

∞

Chuck Wheeler is a sergeant with the Oklahoma City Police Department.

I followed trails of blood down concrete walls in the Federal Building. In a pile of six people was a coach I recognized. A woman was found who said she couldn't breathe. By the time we got an oxygen mask to her she had died.

One victim was trapped by a slab of concrete against her neck and a desk top below. Both of her ankles were trapped under two slabs of concrete. She could only wave her left arm. Her clothing had been ripped off in her fall from the fifth floor to what was once the second floor. She couldn't feel her body — she kept slapping her left leg with the bone sticking out of it. I held her hand to keep her calm. We talked, but her words were muffled by the concrete sur-

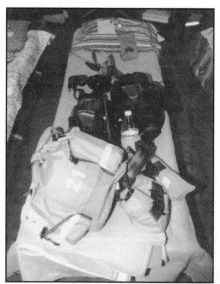

A rescue worker's cot, recently adorned with candy and greetings sent by the nation's children.
— **Photo courtesy of FEMA**

Search teams ascend the twisted pile of the Federal Building's collapsed flooring.
— **Photo courtesy of FEMA**

rounding her. After an hour of holding her hand and talking with her, I was ordered out of the building because I wasn't in protective gear.

I later heard the woman was freed after four hours and survived.

∾

Paul Huber is a firefighter and EMT with the Clinton-Sherman Crash and Fire Rescue Unit in Burns Flat, Oklahoma.

Before April 19 I never even knew the Federal Building existed. I knew I would see some things in my work, but I never thought I would see what I did on this day of April and days, weeks, even months afterward.

Our crew had just finished breakfast when we heard the Weatherford, Oklahoma, Fire Department had been called out. Pretty soon ambulances from all over were responding, and we thought there had been a terrible wreck, so we moved to the alarm room and listened for more information. We flipped on the TV, and to our shock and horror we saw the building, torn and mangled, filling the screen. It looked like a scene from the Middle East.

My lieutenant left the room, then returned fifteen minutes later and told me and fireman James Glover to hook up our cascade trailer to a pickup. We loaded the truck with bars, axes, rope, airpacks, trauma kits, gloves, bunker gear, and fuel. We left around 12:30 P.M. and got to Oklahoma City about an hour and a half later. The urge to get in there, to dig for survivors, and to help as many people as possible had our adrenaline pumping.

Glass and concrete was everywhere. Rebar hung out of the building. It looked as if a giant hand had just pushed in the roof and smashed the whole building down. We were sent to a staging area, where we checked in. We were given flashlights, gloves, and hard hats, but because of various reasons that were unclear to us, the FBI, ATF, and others would not let us in. We left our location after five or six hours and returned to the command post. Finally, an officer with the Oklahoma City Fire Department called us over to the command truck to thank us and tell us we could go home, as they already had plenty of help.

So we went on home, neither of us saying much. We were upset, and wondering. We had desperately wanted to help, and I couldn't help feeling useless. It's as if I never accomplished a thing. While there, I saw the faces of fear, sorrow, and emptiness. I also saw faces of pride. Although my emotions about it are mixed, I still love my job. It calls me to help people, and I would do anything for anyone.

∞

Brian Rhodes is a paramedic for EMSA, Oklahoma City's ambulance service.

We parked at 6th and Robinson, in front of the Journal Record Building. I felt like I was watching one of those 1970s disaster movies. Over the next six hours I helped triage countless victims, ducked two more bomb scares, and probably circled the building a hundred times in the process.

Around 3:30 P.M. I returned to EMSA headquarters. I felt like I had handled the experience pretty well. I didn't realize how emotionally affected I was until I returned to my car and was approached by a young man. He asked me if I had been to the building and I told him that I had. His eyes were bloodshot and swollen and his voice began to shake as he asked, "I'm only asking because my wife works there. Is it bad?" I tried to think of some words of comfort or hope, but all that came out was, "Yeah, it's bad."

∞

Penny Turpen James is a forensic photographer attached to the Will Rogers World Airport Rescue and Fire Department. She arrived on site at 9:35 A.M.

69

I stood on the corner of 5th and Harvey, looking toward the southeast. A few cars in the parking lot across the street were still doing a slow burn. Two injured victims were visible inside the Murrah Building. One man was standing very near the edge of the remaining floor, where it dropped straight off. The right side of his face was bloody, but he stood tall, staring across the street to the Journal Record Building. He seemd to be in shock, and I was relieved to see some rescuers edging toward him. I snapped his picture, and now every time I look at it I wonder who he is and how he is doing.

I wasn't after front page photos, so I got on with the job of recording evidence. I photographed the shrapnel-holed hulks that were once cars, the broken windows blocks away, and pieces of shattered building crunching under foot. Gurneys were wheeled by. The injured sat on the curb, waiting to be bandaged, and occasionally an acquaintance hurried by, pausing just long enough to ask how I was. One of them mentioned the date. I didn't make the connection. "Waco," he said. "Two years ago today." I felt a fist squeeze my heart.

An Ozarka water truck appeared. Four delivery men jumped out and, without a word, stacked cases of bottled water on all four street corners. As the day wore on, I found water on every corner I passed.

Later, at a Critical Incident Stress Debriefer, I talked to many of the rescuers who spent time in the building. One rescue worker told of watching a bird build a nest in a shattered traffic light hanging above the intersection of 5th and Harvey. I wondered when our rebuilding would begin.

cn

Earl Faubion is an Oklahoma City Police sergeant.

I noticed a young man in civilian clothes wandering around aimlessly. Upon inquiring, I was told he had been involved with the rescue effort and was traumatized. I approached him and he said he had carried dead babies out of the building. His car was somewhere downtown, but he didn't know exactly where, nor did he seem to care, so I offered to drive him in an effort to find it. We ended up heading for his parents' place of business in the southwest part of the city. I did my best to try and ease the pain I knew he was feeling, but I doubt if he heard much of what I said. After dropping him off, I returned to the site. I don't know what became of him.

I joined a bucket brigade. I was at the end of the line, and it was just grab-and-toss, grab-and-toss. The rubber gloves on my hands soon ripped apart. A call for flashlights went out, and we were told we were going inside, but before we could enter we were turned back. The person they wanted us to help had been declared dead and that part of the building was determined to be too unsafe to access.

A few minutes later several firemen brought out a woman on a stretcher. I couldn't tell if she was dead or not. A ghostly figure then wandered past me. It took a minute to realize it was Sergeant Dan Helmuth. His uniform was covered head to toe with powdery ash. I walked with him for a minute. "Dan, are you okay?" I asked. "Yeah," he replied. I pointed to a large bloodstain on his left sleeve. "Is this yours?" He said it wasn't. I saw that thousand-yard stare in his eyes, as he continued walking on aimlessly.

I looked down at my own uniform and felt ashamed because it was so much cleaner than Dan's. Later, when I returned home, I was greeted by my wife Charlotte. All I could do was mutter about dead babies and cry. Outside, it had started to rain.

∞

Senior Airman A. J. Haines is assigned to the 72nd Security Police Squadron at Tinker Air Force Base, as an explosive detector dog handler.

When I was told a building downtown had blown up, I

went straight to the kennels to get my dog Reno. As an explosive dog handler, I often go on bomb threats off base to assist the County Bomb Squad, so I had no reason to expect anything big.

I was with the kennelmaster. We found an Oklahoma City Police Officer who tried to locate the bomb squad for us. There were a few medics on the scene and many firefighters and police officers who were covered with blood from treating the injured. They yelled for bandages and blankets, so we gave them everything we had in our first-aid kit.

The captain of the bomb squad appeared and told me he wanted the cars along the street searched for any possible explosives. I began to search cars that looked like crushed soda cans and quickly discovered the ground was blanketed in glass, like a light dusting of snow. With no safe place to walk, I was worried about Reno's paws. I just hoped his pads were tough enough and kept on searching.

I was told to clear out a post office that had taken extensive damage. The entire south wall was nearly gone. I went inside and was met by a postal worker. He had been badly cut, and his shirt was soaked red. His head was nearly covered with a makeshift bandage that covered one eye. I tried to get him to leave, but he insisted that he had to stay because the mail was federal property and there was no one else to take responsibility for it.

Reno and I searched several other locations that day, including the State Capitol. The damage I saw was worse than any hurricane I have seen back east.

By late afternoon, Reno and I were exhausted and ravenous, so we returned to the original parking lot where we had begun. A truck pulled up beside me and a lady asked me if I was hungry. She offered me a Sonic hamburger, which I readily accepted as I thanked her for her thoughtfulness. She said I deserved the thanks. Within minutes I was offered pizza from Godfather's and sandwiches from someone else, and finally some bottled water. Groups of people offered us everything they had to give.

I remained posted downtown until the day the building was razed. During that whole time, the people of Oklahoma

Rescue crews dig
through the rubble,
one handful at a time.
— **Photo courtesy of
FEMA**

Rescuers examine one
of hundreds of hidden
pockets within the
building's remains.
— **Photo courtesy of FEMA**

selflessly offered me whatever I or my dog needed. Everything from good food to boots for Reno's feet, it was all there.

ග

Police Sergeant Kevin Thompson was involved in the initial stage of the day's most dramatic rescue.

We returned to the basement area, where a lady was still trapped. The firemen had removed enough concrete so we could see the girl's face. Her name was Daina, and I crawled in until we were face to face. I said, "It's great to see you, Daina. Hang on, because it won't be much longer." She said she was cold. She didn't know her leg was crushed. I asked her if she felt like anything was broken and she said, "No, I just can't get out." She was calm but saturated with the cold water. A doctor took over, and after assessing her condition it was decided the only way to get her out alive was to amputate her leg.

Several things have changed in my life since that day. I have a new respect for firemen and for women. Also, as a police officer, I see mostly the ugly side of people, and I had come to believe that most people in our world are bad. I now take great comfort in the fact that so many citizens that day proved me wrong.

ග

Oklahoma City Police Sergeant Ronnie Burks is a member of the K-9 Unit.

We couldn't take the K-9s in initially because of the instability of the building, so we rushed in without them to help pull people out. In the basement area firefighters were attempting to assist a young woman, later known as Daina

Bradley, who was pinned under a large block of concrete. Her leg was crushed under a beam which also supported the floor that had been directly over her. Water was rising and the support beam right over us was severely cracked. Blood from victims somewhere overhead ran down the side of one wall.

A water pump was brought down by the electric company and I was given a quick lesson on how to operate the thing by one of their people. A city engineer came by and told us that the concrete beam and flooring were capable of coming down and that we'd better shore it up quick with whatever we could find. We began piling rocks and lengths of steel under the beam. The engineer told me to put my hand on it and monitor any vibrations I felt.

We could all have been buried alive at any second, but for the time all we could think about was getting Miss Bradley out. When the second bomb scare came, I will never forget the look on her face when she was told we would have to leave. She pleaded, "Please don't leave me."

I have been a police officer for twelve years, and I always follow orders, but leaving that young woman under those conditions is the biggest regret I've had. Given another opportunity, that is one order I would disobey. Thankfully, she was eventually extracted and survived. Later, and in the following days, my dog Arlo and I maneuvered throughout the building to find and mark the locations of those who did not survive.

∽

Keith Bryan is fire chief for the City of Nichols Hills, an Oklahoma City suburb.

Blood and glass were everywhere. As we entered the basement we were met by a Highway Patrol Trooper. He was carrying a woman who had been maimed by shrapnel from the building — small chunks of concrete hurled by the blast. Later I noticed the large holes blown in the vehicles across the street. It looked like someone had taken a shotgun loaded with slugs and buckshot and just started shooting everything in sight until there was nothing left to destroy.

The basement was dark. Water flowed from ruptured mains into the lower levels, where it was already boot high. Everything that was once on the ceiling was now on the floor, and electrical wires were slung around loose and live, sparking into the water. Walking through was like climbing a mountain. Crumbled rocks rattled beneath our boots and briar thickets of wires grabbed at us with each step. We fell constantly, getting tangled in the maze of wires as we struggled to get up and continue on.

The pattern we discovered was that whenever we found a large hump in the mangled mess, we usually found a desk. Each time we found a desk, we would try to clear it to the extent we could, hoping to find a survivor, but afraid we would find a body instead. As we searched, we saw pictures of families and friends of the victims float by in the rising water.

A firefighter yelled, "I've got one!" Everybody converged. We found a woman sitting up in a chair, wedged under her desk. Her legs looked broken and she was in a stupor. As we pulled her out a fireman laid down beside her to hold her head above water. We found a desk top to use as a backboard and carried her toward daylight as quick as we could get there. Only a few feet from where she was found, we saw another woman and a man. Both were dead.

Somehow I ended up in the parking garage. I met a firefighter there who said there was a lady trapped nearby. All I could see was a tunnel formed by large beams and collapsed sections of flooring. The firefighter said, "Daina, raise your hand." Through a hole no larger than a Kleenex box I saw a hand move weakly.

Sergeant Ron Stone yelled, "Chief, we found another one!" This one was spotted through a hole in the rubble about the size of a computer monitor. She told us her name was Terri. Firefighter Chris Crane and Ron Stone worked on trying to remove her, while others tried to move the concrete trapping Daina. Then the order to evacuate was sounded at the suspicion of another bomb.

I told everyone to listen up, but to continue working. I asked the workers how long it would take to free Daina, and was told it would be a while. I ordered them to leave, then turned to Chris and Ron and asked how long it would take to get Terri out. Chris answered, "Four or five minutes, tops." I asked if they wanted to stay. Both said yes.

Terri and Daina overheard all this and began crying, "Don't leave me." After cutting through the steel and concrete trapping Terri, Chris and Ron told her the only way they could get her out was to pull her through the small abrasive opening. They told her it would hurt. "Pull!" she said without hesitation. Terri was successfully removed. She had suffered severe injuries to her legs and arms.

Four people now remained in the parking garage. Besides myself there was Chief Mike Shannon, Daina, and another trapped victim we had not yet reached. Daina was crying out, "Don't leave me!" Mike reached in to touch her, promising her that we'd be back with more equipment. As we turned to leave, I started to cry myself.

I walked out of the garage and found the streets empty, but I was too emotionally drained and too tired to run. I walked away from the building and from Daina slowly, feeling absolutely hollow inside.

∽

Orthopedic surgeon Andy Sullivan crawled deep into the creaking building to heroically perform the most dramatic operation of his career.

I was in my clinic watching the coverage on TV when Dr. David Tuggle called to inform me that a victim had been found alive, trapped by a concrete beam. By his analysis, the only way she could be saved was to amputate her leg.

I immediately ran to the operating room and obtained an amputation set, four disposable scalpels, and cut some nylon traction rope to be used as a tourniquet. I borrowed tennis shoes from one of the hospital orderlies and left all my other belongings except my drivers license to carry for identification.

I then ran to the emergency room, where a policeman for the hospital drove me to the site. Once at the building, I inquired as to the whereabouts of Dr. Tuggle. I was led to a stairwell that descended to the basement area of the building. From there, I climbed down a ladder into a cavernous hole, where the floor was strewn with broken concrete sitting in water. The sound of a generator running in the distance for light and electricity drew us to the spot where firemen were intently working to gain access to the trapped victim.

The lady, Daina Bradley, whom I knew then only as Daina, lay at the end of a long crevice. It was very much like exploring a cave or climbing into a rock cavern. A huge beam of concrete had fallen on top of her, along her right side, landing at her right knee and partially hitting her right arm. At least one upper floor was pressed against the beam, pinning everything tight. Her right arm had been freed by the rescuers. She was on her back in approximately six inches of water. The space was such that to gain access to her required getting on your belly and crawling in. Only one person at a time could fit in the space. The floor overlaying her was so unstable, one of the rescuers was holding his hand on the beam to feel for movement.

After surveying the situation closely, it was obvious that Daina's leg was destroyed below the knee. Even if it were extracted it would be lost. Any tampering with the beam could be catastrophic. The only solution was to amputate the leg in order to get her out. To access it, I had to lay right on top of her. As I made preparations, another bomb scare was sounded and we had to pull out. We hated to leave her, but the time was used to further plan an approach when we went back in.

When we returned, I realized I couldn't quite reach her knee, and there wasn't space to do a mid-thigh amputation, which would require cutting through the femur. Blocking my access to her knee was a large piece of reinforced steel. The firemen had to crawl back in with a power saw and cut

Left:
Search teams
prepare to enter the
Murrah Building for
another shift.
— **Photo courtesy of
FEMA**

Below:
Workers use heavy
equipment to break
up a concrete slab.
— **Photo courtesy of
FEMA**

away the steel, which was only accomplished after more critical time went by. I slithered back in, positioned myself on top of her, and was able to reach the knee joint with my left hand. My plan was to go through the knee.

The firemen positioned a harness under her chest so that once the amputation was completed she could be rapidly pulled out and onto a spine board for removal. This would also help us control bleeding, if it became excessive.

I discussed all this with the patient, explaining it was our only choice. She was tearful and obviously afraid, but she understood the absolute necessity of it. Though I didn't verbalize it, I was also afraid she would not survive much longer, as she was already hypothermic and her breathing was labored.

I backed out long enough to get the disposable knives, then began cutting off her jeans. I applied the tourniquets and cut through the knee as quickly as possible. When it was done, the rescuers were able to pull her out to the spine board and evacuate her to a part of the basement where we could look at the amputation site and place clamps to control bleeding. A bandage was applied, then we moved out through the parking garage to a waiting ambulance, where she was transported to University Hospital. She was stabilized in the emergency room and was later taken to surgery for additional wound care. During her hospitalization I learned that Daina had lost her mother and two daughters in the blast, and that a sister had been injured as well.

Even though physicians are trained to isolate themselves emotionally from patients and to be decisive and action oriented, making the decision to do this was difficult. It is an experience that will be vivid in my memory forever.

∞

Sergeant Kevin McCullough is an EMT with the Oklahoma City Police Department.

I had checked out an ambulance and was on my way to give a presentation to my daughter's home school support group when the EMSA radio announced what had happened.

I phoned dispatch and advised that I could respond. I then phoned my wife, Kathy, and told her I wouldn't be able to make the presentation. I was concerned, because Kathy was due with our fourth child any day.

I picked up a partner and headed to the scene. We immediately started transporting victims. We made many trips to and from the hospital. The last patient we transported was a young lady whose leg had been amputated at the bomb site.

After delivering the last victim, my pager went off. I dialed the unfamiliar number and my daughter answered. While I'd been in the midst of this incredible death and destruction, my wife had delivered our son, Jordan.

∽

Margaret Durham is a licensed professional counselor with the Child Guidance Services Office of the Cleveland County Health Department.

During the second bomb scare, we were crossing a field or unpaved area next to an industrial building. A small nest filled with tiny eggs was discovered in the middle of this field. It had been pointed out to our group by a mother bird that was squawking and chirping an alarm. People started shouting, "Watch out for the nest, there are eggs, watch out!" Emotions for all were running high, and the urgency to save these eggs was evident. A few stones were placed by the nest to identify the area and we began to walk in a wide path so no harm would be done to those precious, fragile eggs.

When we returned, a nurse in a long white coat began organizing volunteers in groups to head to the building. As we approached, I noticed a man sitting on a curb with his head down, sobbing. I went over to him as the group moved on. A nurse, whom I did not know, also approached the man. We sat down to talk to him. His name was Bill. He began telling me about a woman named Daina that he had been helping rescue workers with. He kept saying over and over, "I don't even know her last name. I just want to know she's all right. They haven't gotten her out yet. They may have to amputate her leg." His compassion for this woman, a total stranger, was overwhelming.

Bill had been in Oklahoma City a short time. He had been living close to downtown and the explosion had thrown him out of his bed. He had raced to the site to help any way he could. He was now covered with water and mud. He wanted to go back, but he had been told to rest. As he described the morgue that had hastily been set up, the grief he expressed made us all start crying.

Two men came over as we continued to talk and comfort each other. One was a fireman and the other a physician. They began to pat him on the back and praise him. The doctor asked me, "Do you know this man?" I replied, "No, I've just met him today." The physician continued, "Well, you need to know this man. He is a real hero."

I saw Bill two other times that day, and spoke with him each time. He was supposed to have gone home, but he could not leave.

∽

Oklahoma City Police Lieutenant David Simpson led the Emergency Response Team into the bomb site to secure the perimeter.

We had studied the World Trade Center bombing. We knew which mistakes to avoid. In New York it was two days before perimeters were set and a lot of evidence was lost. Ambulances and emergency personnel couldn't get close to the area.

We knew to keep all traffic out. Our guys in mobile units knew to park out of the way to keep the area clear. Intersections were roped off and all vehicles were stopped except for fire engines, ambulances, cranes, and things like gas company vehicles. Everybody else was on foot.

This was the largest crime scene, the worst mass murder in the history of America. Security was tight. We had great help from the National Guard. Cops came in from all over the state and country. They didn't get the opportunity to do all the high profile work, but without them we'd have been up to our eyebrows in media or guys looking for souvenirs.

Business owners would call us wanting to get into their businesses to check on things. We couldn't let them, but I could assure them that nothing had been taken. The Federal Reserve Bank had been evacuated, and when they returned, not a dime was missing.

It wasn't always easy to keep people out. One angry man was determined to get past the tape and into the building. His daughter was one of the missing. I told him that I had a child and that I could only imagine a little bit of what he was feeling, but that the building was too unstable and dangerous. I couldn't let him risk his life and the lives of the rescue workers. Eventually, his daughter's body was recovered. Days later he came back to thank me for the job I'd done.

∞

Joshua Cole, an eighteen-year-old civilian with only slight medical training, rushed to the scene with his mother, Bobbie Cole, from their office four miles away, and soon found himself immersed in some of the most horrifying aspects of the disaster.

I worked during high school as a volunteer for the police department and had some medical training in a mental institution. We went to the triage area, where for the first few hours we moved people from one place to the next, trying to hold their bodies intact and helping those we could,

83

while trying to ignore the awful specter of those we could not. At some point I was asked by some nurses to go with them to the building. When I first stood next to it, I was stunned. The loud and constant drone of sirens, voices, and rescue machinery faded into nothing and there was an impossible silence. Every sense I had came alive in the presence of so much death.

A thousand odors clung to the air and to my clothes. For a moment, I thought I also sensed the smell of fear, and oddly enough, guilt. I could hear high above me something swinging and creaking; probably a piece of the building, but it sounded almost as if the building itself was crying in pain as its torn walls managed to hold on by the thinnest of metal threads. I could see the charred remains of the building and pieces of people so small and ragged you could easily pass over them if you didn't know what you were looking for. Most of the medical waste had already been cleared away and placed into large orange bags proclaiming them as biohazard.

Later, I ran errands for the various law enforcement and safety officials. There was a staggering amount of radio use, so it was next to impossible to sort out anything that wasn't directly aimed at you. I volunteered to hand deliver requests for supplies and other information. After a time I was stopped and asked why I was running around so close to the site, and a fireman nearby told the officer flatly that I was being allowed to because I was the only person they had found who had been to all the command posts and knew where everything was. After a while, everyone called me "Kid."

I was there ten or twelve hours total. I don't know how I made it without becoming violently sick or numb with emotion. Once I was home, it hit me all at once. My mother went to bed, and I went to my room and cried for a long time. I was very difficult to be around for a while afterward. A sense of rage threatened to explode. I also felt deep sorrow for those who had suffered, admiration for those who had helped, and anger when hearing people who were not there talk about it. That may be selfish, but it was true. It is a similar reaction, I have been told, to discussing the Vietnam

Left:
A ladder is bolted to the building's broken flooring to create additional access.
—Photo courtesy of Steve Fayfitch

Below:
A shattered signal light hangs in silence at a nearby intersection.
— Photo courtesy of David Allen

War with a veteran from that era. You just cannot imagine what it was like unless you were there.

Even so, it affected us all, whether we were there or not, and if we have feelings for those who died, be they intimately close to us or strangers, then we will all mourn. If we look upon the dead and the dying, a piece of us has died. If we look upon the faces and bodies of those who did not die, then we are all scarred. Most importantly, if we all have hope, then we are all survivors.

∽

Steven Powell is an employee of a Tulsa manufacturing firm and vice-president of Search and Rescue Dogs of Oklahoma, Inc.

Bronte, my search dog, and I saw things that day no person should ever see. The inside of the building was surreal. I walked over to the mouth of a cave-like entrance to the first floor. The opening was six feet by twelve feet, triangular shaped with a forty-five-degree angled roof or concrete hanging by rebar. It literally looked like it could swallow you.

The wreckage determined our path. I gazed up through holes that a man could easily fall through, veiled by loose debris. Nothing was recognizable. We cautiously walked and crawled, with no idea how many floors were beneath us, or if we were going to fall through at any second. We searched and searched. Twice Bronte alerted, at 6:05 and 6:25 P.M. When Bronte alerted three times to the same pile of rubble, I knew we had something. Noise from generators and the elevator alarm was deafening, though, and I couldn't have heard a survivor cry out. But I suspected Bronte did.

There were no firefighters around, so we left to go find an excavation crew. My partner told the firefighters that we thought Bronte had something down there. We both told them where the alerts had taken place. They sent a crew in immediately to begin searching. Bronte was exhausted, so we left the building. About thirty minutes later the dog liaison officer of the Sheriff's Office came up to us and said, "One of your dogs found four people alive!" I asked where, and he said it was on the first floor near the stairwell. I knew Bronte had found them because it was our assigned area. About an hour later, he came back and told us that only one had actually survived. The other three were found dead.

Around 10:00 P.M. I watched from only a few feet away as medical personnel carried out Brandy Liggons, who would become the very last survivor.

∽

Theda Adkisson works for the State of Oklahoma and is a volunteer with the Choctaw, Oklahoma, Fire Department.

I was with fellow volunteer Bob Burton. About 7:00 P.M. we were stretching cord for lights, one set of which was placed at the top of the stairwell we were in. Someone had been in with a dog to search. Bob was at the landing and noticed a jacket. I walked up the stairs and we shined our lights into the large opening where the wall on the east side of the staircase had been blown away. I could see the jacket, too. It was covered with dust. Bob asked if I thought there was someone in the jacket. I said I didn't think so, since it had been such a warm day and this was a winter jacket.

We kept looking. Bob thought the area had been a restroom since it had tile on the wall. He walked down the stairs, out of sight to investigate further with his flashlight. My husband, Allen, who is also a fireman, was on the scene with us. He walked up to Bob, who showed him the coat. They decided Allen would crawl in and check the coat with the understanding that if he felt it was unsafe he would exit. They made the opening a little larger, then Allen crawled in past the opening where I was standing, and checked the jacket. The building appeared stable, so he worked his way into the restroom area, and that's where he found the victim.

87

He told us to be quiet, then asked, "Do you hear me?" We thought he was talking to us and we started to answer back. Allen yelled, "Shut up! I think I hear someone." At that point, Bob went into the hole, and shortly afterward Jerry McKee, another fireman, entered also. I started in through the staircase hole, and was barely in when I heard a female voice. Allen said, "Keep talking so we can find you." He asked me to relay to the outside that we had found someone alive.

Soon a firefighter, a paramedic, and Dr. Rick Nelson were on their way in. Dr. Nelson was dressed in surgical scrubs and asked me to lead him in. I told the guys we had a doctor, a paramedic, and a backboard for the rescue. I held my flashlight for them. I could hear them talking to the young lady. Allen, Bob, and Jerry were removing concrete piece by piece. Jerry had uncovered the only portion of her body visible, her feet. When he squeezed her toes, he asked if this was her foot. She told him "yes," and wiggled her toes. Bob asked, "What is your name?" She replied, "Brandy. Would you hurry and get me out of here?" He told her, "We're having to move a lot of stuff and it will take a little while. I have a niece named Brandy. How old are you?" She said she was fifteen. Bob kept talking to her to keep her calm.

Dr. Nelson crawled up close to her and introduced himself. He told Brandy he was the best looking doctor in Oklahoma. He talked to her, reassuring her while explaining that it would take a little time. Allen passed the larger hunks from around her head to me while Bob was by her waist removing concrete, rebar and conduit as fast as he could. Jerry was working near her feet, and all of them took turns talking to her. Bolt cutters were brought in, as well as saws and other equipment.

Allen had been lying on his stomach for about forty-five minutes, digging in earnest, when he turned to Bob and said, "I've got a cramp. Do you want to move up by her head for a while?" The space by her head was like a triangle that became more and more narrow. Brandy was positioned right at an overhang, where large pieces of concrete were suspended over the edges of the upper floors.

Dr. Nelson moved into Bob's position. At some point a hole was finally made large enough for Bob to reach in, and Brandy felt his hand. She clinched it tight and didn't want to let go. An hour and a half later, another firefighter came in and said, "I want everybody out of here except OK City." I turned to leave and Allen began slowly moving in the same direction. Being ordered out upset Bob, as he did not want to let go of Brandy's hand.

When they finally got her out, we were all waiting, using our flashlights to make a lighted pathway to the outside. When Brandy reached the gurney outside, Bob and Jerry spoke to her. She was in critical condition, but was alert and talking. Like us, Brandy Liggons had no way of knowing then that she would be the last to be taken alive from the decimated building.

With the specter of the Federal Building as a backdrop, Governor Frank Keating (wearing hard hat) confers with police and fire officials in this unintentional double exposure.

— Photo courtesy of David Allen

Above: Workers proceed with the tedious task of moving the rubble.   **— Photo courtesy of FEMA**

Below: FEMA Urban Search and Rescue team members from California take a breather.
— Photo courtesy of Oscar Johnson

PART

II

Survivors

I hung up the phone and all the lights went off. I saw a small flash, probably from my computer screen, and heard a woman say, "Oh!" — like the surprised "oh" people say when the power goes off.

Florence Rogers is the chief executive officer of the Federal Employees Credit Union, which occupied the center of the Murrah Building's third floor.

It felt like a whirling tornado hit, turning and twisting me and the chair. I never heard an explosion, although there was a lot of noise like in an Oklahoma windstorm.

"What on earth is happening? This is like a bad movie, and when all this stuff stops I'm going to get out of here," I thought. I never considered for a moment that I might die.

I was sucked out of the chair and slammed against the floor and wall under the credenza — only now the credenza was standing on end and there was a cement pillar where I'd been sitting. A steel beam lay right beside me and piles of debris were everywhere. I could see blue sky instead of walls and ceilings. I kind of twisted around and looked out the window, noticing the glass was gone, and yelled for help.

I never lost consciousness, but it was sure all mixed up. I turned back around and looked for my desk and for my people.

There was only a narrow ledge along the south wall of what had been our part of the third floor. That was all that was left. The rest was completely gone.

Just outside my window the building structure extended in a "U" shape, which was an enclosed back stairwell. Two firemen appeared in the window to my right, and they yelled at me to stay calm. I noticed the glass was also gone from that window.

I considered jumping from the window down to the plaza. I stepped gingerly out on that slanting window ledge, testing its strength. Even though the metal trim had been loosened in the blast, it felt fairly sturdy.

The two firemen leaned out their window and their four hands grabbed my two, pulling me up into the stairwell. They helped me through the debris down two flights to the plaza.

∽

Terry Rose works for Oklahoma Natural Gas Company (ONG) downtown. His mother and stepfather, Florence and Dan Rogers, were inside the Murrah Building at 9:02 A.M.

Our own building absorbed part of the blast. I ran down four flights of stairs under falling ceiling tiles and crumbling pieces of who-knows-what. Within two minutes I was climbing the steps of the plaza outside the south side of the Federal Building. I could see blue sky all the way through the building. Bleeding people were all over. I saw a woman who couldn't walk being pushed down the street in a chair.

I returned to the ONG offices and found a man in the lobby who had hobbled in from the third floor of the Murrah Building. His office had been near my mom's. He was talking to his wife on the phone. I hung on every word of his conversation, then spent the next two hours taking this man to meet his wife. We introduced ourselves only when we finally arrived.

Back at the blast area I was told all family members were to gather at the corner of Harvey and 6th Street. After a while I heard my name being yelled. I turned and saw Jerry Bowers, a mechanical contractor I've worked with through ONG, running toward me. "Oh, Jerry, my mom is in the credit union, and I don't know if she's okay."

"Terry, my wife works in the Social Security office," he answered. We held on to each other, like brothers, united by a common bond.

During the confusion I found my stepfather's secretary, and she told me he was outside the building, helping to recover injured. So far so good, but she had no word on mom. I convinced Jerry that we should go to St. Anthony Hospital, so we walked there. On the way he used my cellular phone to check with his family to see if they had heard from his wife, Carol. Nothing.

In the basement of the hospital lists of names on the wall began to grow. Every time the nurse added names, Jerry and I would search them immediately. Still nothing. At 1:30

my pager sounded. The number was one I didn't recognize. When I called I was put on hold. Then I heard the voice that so many mornings had awakened me as a child. It was mom saying "hello."

I fell into a chair and began to sob. People around me drew close and I had to turn from the telephone to tell them mom was all right. I had to leave to get her and take her to a doctor, and that meant leaving my friend Jerry behind. He grabbed me around the neck and urged to go take care of my mom. We both prayed a short prayer for his wife Carol.

Mom was banged up, but the doctor deemed her in excellent condition, considering what she'd been through, and sent her home. She began to cry when we got there. Together we called the families of her fellow employees and were able to account for thirteen that were either not at work or had been able to escape. That left eighteen in the credit union missing. We passed the information on to the FBI, then I took mom to a disaster recovery meeting that afternoon.

That night we made calls to apartment managers, asking them to check on animals and children that might be home alone and needing assistance. Everyone was willing to do whatever we asked. My aunt Jo arrived, and over the next four days she answered 561 calls.

I attended six funerals in the next week, making me even more aware of how lucky my family had been. My friend Jerry Bowers hadn't been as lucky. We buried his wife, Carol, on Tuesday. There we embraced once again, sharing that bond developed on the morning of April 19.

cn

Richard Dean is a claims representative for the Social Security Administration.

I remember a brilliant flash of light and the sensation of an invisible force pressing me out of my chair and to my knees before everything turned pitch black. I found myself covered with bulky five-foot square ceiling tiles, shattered

Above: Heavy illumination allowed search operations to continue around the clock. **—— Photo courtesy of David Allen**

Below: Construction cranes assist in efforts to stabilize the decimated building. **— Photo courtesy of Oscar Johnson**

glass from light fixtures, modular furniture panels, and overhead doors from my modular credenza unit which had sheared off and hit me in the back. My immediate concern was my ability to see. I thought my eyes were wide open, but they were not adjusting to the darkness. Breathing was also difficult due to the dust. While groping for anything familiar, I could hear the cries of individuals trying to free themselves over the roar of what sounded like sliding gravel being dumped from a truck. The cries for help from the front office and the sound of the collapsing upper floors stopped simultaneously.

I located Sharon Littlejohn, who had been standing in the front of the office. The force of the explosion had blown her forty feet back from the reception area. She was under three to four feet of rubble. Her outer clothing had been blown off and she was completely soaked with blood and water. She was barely recognizable due to significant blood loss in the scalp and facial area. She also complained she was not able to breathe. It was apparent I couldn't get her out by myself, because of her extensive injuries, so I explained to her I needed help to get her out. I went to the rear of the office, where I found Sgt. Richard Williams and Sgt. Keith Simonds of the Oklahoma City Police Department. It took all three of us to carry her out, due to the debris we had to climb over and through.

∽

Jandra Mayer is a nursing student at the University of Oklahoma and volunteered following the explosion.

All the alarms in the hospital were going off. The fire alarm was sounding, which required us to shut all the doors to the patients' rooms. The new mothers were wondering what had just happened, also. All we could do was tell them we didn't know, but we would try to find out.

Within minutes someone spotted the smoke coming

from the downtown area less than two blocks away. We turned on the television, which already had live coverage.

∞

Registered Nurse Kathy Vierling works at University Hospital, only a short distance from the Federal Building.

I was on the phone with a nurse in the ICU, in the process of giving a slow, detailed report on a patient that I would be bringing up soon. It was as if something hit the side of the building. The back doors flew open and then slammed shut.

I ran outside. There were car alarms going off everywhere. I went back inside and picked up the phone. About this time part of the transmission came through on the ambulance encoder. It was unclear who they were talking to, and all we caught was "Big explosions, expect mass casualties!" I grabbed my paperwork and yelled at the EMT student working with me that day, "Let's get upstairs!" I have never moved O2 equipment, monitors, and IV pumps so fast in my life.

As we were running down the hallway, I remarked to the EMT student with me, "This will be an experience of a lifetime. Won't you have something to share back at school." He agreed, saying all he had hoped for was an interesting day.

∞

Barry Fogerty is a survivor from the Oklahoma Water Resources Board Building.

One of my co-workers, Mike McGaugh, regained consciousness ten minutes after the blast and wondered why he was lying down with his feet in sunlight. He found me stretched across a drafting table with my legs pinned under me. He tried to get me out, but couldn't.

He went to a rather large hole in the south wall of the building and began calling for help. He eventually got the attention of an emergency worker who told him they were on their way. Mike said the face of the fireman that showed up was that of a human male, but definitely looked like an angel.

The fireman extracted me from the mess and put a neck brace and hood bandage over my head. An EMT started medical treatment in the parking lot. Mike rode with me to the hospital and made calls to my family. Three doctors spent three and a half hours cleaning and stitching my wounds. Two surgeries were required to get glass out of my back. I also had hearing, balance, and neurology problems.

In spite of it, I was able to attend my son's graduation from the University of Oklahoma on May 13, one day after doctors took a one-and-a-half by three-quarter-inch piece of glass out of my shoulder. I had worked long and hard to see him graduate, and I got to do it. I was kind of wobbly, though.

∽

Donna Abla was substitute teaching at Liberty Academy in Shawnee, Oklahoma, on April 19.

Suddenly, the phone rang and, before I could speak, a man's voice sounded in my ear. "Someone blew up the Federal Building!"

"What?" I said, thinking that whoever was calling was out of his mind.

"Half of the Federal Building is gone!" he yelled in my ear. In the background I could hear a lot of noise and as he told me his name I knew he was not crazy. He was calling the church office to let us know that his wife had made it out from the seventh floor with only minor cuts and bruises.

Their daughter was a student at Liberty Academy, a private church school where I was working on April 19, 1995. Without thinking, I grabbed a yellow legal pad and wrote down their names and their daughter's name. I hung up the

phone just long enough to tell another secretary that someone had blown up the Federal Building, when the phone
rang again.

This time it was one of our church members. She was in
Oklahoma City looking out her window and crying. She
asked me to let the church know that at least one of the
people in her office had a daughter working in the Social
Security Office on a temporary job. The mother had not yet
heard from her. I quickly jotted down the name and told her
that we would all pray for the daughter to be found. By this
time someone had turned on a TV and we began to hear the
sickening reports that Oklahoma City had been struck by
terrorism. The phone continued to ring, bringing names of
others who were feared missing. My list soon covered the
front page of the legal pad and I found myself turning to the
next empty page, which would soon be filled with more
names of those we loved.

∽

HUD employee Jane Graham was in a computer class on the Murrah Building's ninth floor at 9:02 A.M.

I was supposed to be on the ninth floor for a class and
had to rush to get there. I entered the classroom, sat down,
and turned on the computer. As I did the bomb exploded.
The building shook and the last thing I remember was looking up to see the roof being blown off. The next thing I
knew I heard a co-worker, Sonja Key, calling my name. She
began pulling debris off me, then told me to get up. I told
her I couldn't, but she kept saying, "You have to. You must
get up and get out of here." And with that she reached down
and helped me up.

The smoke was so thick it burned my lungs. We made
our way out to the hall, where the force of the blast had
hurled a door horizontal into the wall. As we climbed up on
the door to get to the stairwell I fell, hitting the concrete

Top photo:
Final clean-up progresses on one of the Murrah Building's upper floors.
— **Photo courtesy of Oscar Johnson**

Bottom photo:
Flags from many of the rescue workers' states decorate the front of the building.
— **Photo courtesy of David Allen**

floor on my knees. Dazed, I followed others down the stairs. The only thought I had was that someone needed to help the children in the day care. As I came to the second floor, a man was holding the door partially open. I asked if I could go in and help with the babies, and he said no, that everything was being taken care of. Two other co-workers, Jaroy and Kathy, helped me across the street. We tried to phone from the bank there to tell our families we were alive, but the lines were jammed.

My daughter was at her home having coffee when the news broke and she saw the pictures on TV. She started screaming when she saw the gaping hole where my office was supposed to be. She got on the phone to her dad. She told him I was dead, that she was looking at the building and that I couldn't have survived. My husband Bob said there must be some mistake and left immediately to look for me. He found a place to park downtown and started walking. Finally, he saw some co-workers he recognized and they told him I had come out of the building in front of them, so they knew I was alive, but didn't know where I was. Bob continued looking for me for a while longer, then realized it would be best to go home and wait.

My co-workers and I were able to get to Jaroy's car, which was parked several blocks away. We drove over to my son-in-law's business, a couple of miles from the building, and made our calls from there. When I got through to my daughter, she came to get me. When she got me home, my husband was waiting at the door. All we could do was hold each other.

As we begin to put our lives back together, to heal, to learn to trust again, and to reevaluate what is really important in our lives, we will become stronger. Only time can help with the fear of not being safe, of not having control over our lives. We will have to take it one step at a time, and never again take life for granted.

∽

Dianne Mitchell recounts the experience of her husband's parents, Joe and Leigh Mitchell, in the Social Security Office. Joe survived, but Leigh perished.

They had an appointment for 9:00 A.M. to sign up for retirement benefits. Joe wanted to be a traveling evangelist. When he was called in for his interview, Leigh stayed in the waiting room. During the interview Joe was asked some questions he couldn't readily answer, so he went to get Leigh. He was about halfway to the waiting area when the bomb detonated. He was hit with pieces of falling building and was knocked to his knees. He remembers light fixtures hitting him and glass flying all around.

When it was over, the building was dark and he had trouble focusing his eyes. He thought, "I have to get to Leigh. She needs me. I have to help her." He looked in the direction where he had left and all he could see was solid pieces of concrete. Because his vision was impaired, he couldn't see how to get out, so he sat there in pain, wiping blood and asking God to help him and Leigh.

A woman came running by. She asked him, "Are you okay?" and kept on running. He remembers telling her, "I'm okay, but don't go down there. I think some live wires are exposed and you might get hurt." She kept on running anyway, toward some light. He realized she had found a way out, so he started crawling in the same direction.

Joe escaped with some glass in his eye, a cut nose, a punctured eardrum, and numerous cuts and bruises. Leigh was crushed under tons of concrete. The rescuers found her nine days later. She had died instantly.

∽

Michael Reyes is an asset manager for HUD. His father, Antonio, was an equal opportunity specialist at the same agency. Michael survived

***the Murrah Building bombing. His father did
not.***

I hung up the phone and all the lights went off. I saw a
small flash, probably from my computer screen and heard a
woman nearby say, "Oh!" — like the surprised "Oh" people
say when the power goes off. I began to hear rumbling, and
my desk, which is a five-person modular unit, started to
shake. I thought it was an earthquake. Even though I've
never experienced an earthquake first-hand, I instinctively
jumped under my desk for protection. Instead of finding
the floor, however, I found myself falling. On the way down,
I said to myself, "This isn't real . . . This isn't real . . . This
isn't real . . . I don't wanna die . . . I don't wanna die . . . I
don't wanna die!" I never heard the explosion that was
heard for miles around. The fall was over too quickly to be
scary. I'm not a scientist, but I believe I was so close to the
bomb that I was in a vacuum, which prevented me from
hearing the explosion. It may have even slowed my fall.

Below me, I saw what appeared to be piles of white concrete. They seemed to be lit up by a bright light, which was
odd considering there was no power in the building. I don't
remember the sensation of being hit by flying objects, but I
suffered a large cut from my left temple down toward my
chin. This may have occurred when I felt my glasses flip off
my face. At the time my only thought was, "Well, there go
my glasses."

I fell four stories, from the seventh floor to the third. I
saw about six people there who appeared to be uninjured. I
was almost half-buried, standing up and slightly tangled in
the remains of the metal supports from a non-load bearing
wall. I called for help, and people came to my aid. They said
I was bleeding badly. They cleared the rubble away, then
had me lean against a small bookshelf while they cleared a
path for us to leave the building. When a path was cleared,
they helped me walk on a radiator, which was next to where
the south window would have been. I climbed out onto the
ledge, which led to another wall about six feet above the
plaza. Two men there helped me off the wall and to the cor-

ner of 4th Street and Harvey, where I waited for an ambulance.

Sheila Schick had found me on the plaza. I asked her if she had seen my dad. She said, "No, but do you realize what this building looks like?" I asked her to stay, and she said she would not leave me. After what seemed like a very short time, I was placed on a wooden stretcher and given a neck brace. I had lacerations on my face, two large cuts on my back, and many cuts and scrapes all over my body. I was loaded onto a makeshift ambulance, which was actually a small city bus designed for the handicapped, and taken to Southwest Medical Center. I was scared that if I closed my eyes, I would never open them again. I told Sheila, "Don't let me close my eyes." She suggested we sing "One Hundred Bottles of Beer on the Wall." I said, "No, that's too involved. Let's count backwards from one hundred." Even this was a bit much, so when we got to ninety, I suggested she count the odds, and I would count the evens.

∽

Priscilla Salyers worked as an Investigative Assistant for the U.S. Customs office. She survived a four-story fall that left her buried in concrete when the floor beneath her desk collapsed from the detonation.

Paul, one of my very best friends, walked up to my desk and said something. I asked him to repeat it just as the phone rang. Still looking at him, I reached for the phone with my left hand, but before I could get the receiver to my ear I was rocked by a tremendous boom. For an instant we locked eyes, then I felt as if I were having a seizure. Paul's blue eyes were the last thing I saw.

An incredible force pushed me forward and all I could see were white flashing sparkles. Loud wind rushed past my ears. I couldn't understand what was happening, and felt

104

Above: A makeshift memorial in front of the Federal Building pays tribute to the victims. **— Photo courtesy of Debbie Drain**

Below: View of the Murrah Building's collapsed roof, looking eastward. **— Photo courtesy of Oscar Johnson**

embarrassed, wondering what Paul must be thinking. I thought I might be having a heart attack, but there was no pain, then suddenly there was a strong jolt and I thought I'd hit my head on my desk. Everything got real quiet.

I tried to sit up but I couldn't move. I told myself to just be still for a few minutes. I wondered where Paul had gone. I expected he would be trying to help me sit up by now. I tried again, then realized there was something holding me down. I was on my stomach, with my face twisted to the right. My head was wedged tight and I had no luck moving my legs or my right arm. My left arm was free, so I reached up to find my computer. No luck. What I felt was something huge on my head and back. I thought my desk and credenza had fallen on me. I visualized Claude, whose desk is near mine, coming to help Paul get me out. The eerie silence was so loud. What was happening?

I tried to scream, only to discover I could barely breathe. The reality that I was trapped rushed home and I became extremely frightened. I started praying for survival and the will to keep calm. Earthquake victims came to mind. What had I read about them? Some survived days within air pockets, didn't they? With my left hand I began pulling rocks out from under my neck to create more breathing space. Drawing air was difficult. There was so much dust. The piece of gum in my mouth was full of dirt. I tried to spit it out, but my head was wedged so tightly I couldn't. It occurred to me that if I had suffered head injuries and my head began to swell, it would be over. I heard a voice. It was a voice of panic. "This is the child care center. We have a lot of children in here!"

Someone answered the voice. "We're trying to get you out." This only confused me more. The day care center was on the second floor. I was in my office on the fifth floor. I thought maybe the voices were coming through the vent. At least people were there. They would find me. But where were Paul and Claude? I managed to scream for help, but with no response. I felt it would be better to save my energy and focus on staying calm until help arrived. Each time I felt myself slipping toward panic, I prayed for calmness, knowing it was my only chance. I tried very hard not to think about time. I knew that if I thought about time, it would only seem longer.

A man yelled, "There's a live one!" He sounded far away, but I felt relief just the same. In reality he was not far away. I felt his hand take mine, which was visible from the outside, and the peace and comfort that washed over me was indescribable. I heard several other men around me. They were discussing the possibility of getting me out. Someone asked my name. I took a slow deep breath and yelled out my name. He had trouble hearing me and asked me to repeat myself. It took some effort, but I said it once again, as loud as I could. He was to my left side and I was screaming into a giant block of concrete. He asked me if I knew why I was down there, then explained that there had been an explosion in the building.

Though I could tell the men were struggling in their effort to get me out, I had little doubt they would be successful. Then the same man who had given me so much comfort told me they had to leave. I squeezed his hand tight, begging him not to leave. He said they had to go for tools. It didn't make sense. Why couldn't he stay while others got the tools? I cried out and begged him to stay. His voice cracked and he said, "I'm sorry." His hand slipped out of mine and they were gone. The silence was maddening.

It seemed like hours went by and they did not come back. I finally got angry and decided I would just get myself out of this tomb. I tightened every muscle in my body in an effort to move the mountain and free myself. It didn't work. I could feel metal bars all twisted around the area I was encased in. I tried digging the broken chunks out from under me with my free hand. In frustration, I grabbed at them and threw the pieces as hard as I could. My right arm and both legs tingled from lack of circulation. I was convinced that if I could just wiggle my toes I would be okay. I wasn't in pain exactly, but I was very uncomfortable and very hot. I attempted to slip my free arm out of my jacket, but got it caught in the sleeve, so I decided to not make bad things worse.

My mind raced. The men still had not come back. I felt a lump under my stomach and reached down there, thinking it was a rock I could pull out and throw. What I discovered was not a rock, but a woman's hand. I started to cry, praying that whoever it belonged to was not suffering. I took the hand in mine and held it for quite a while.

At some point later I heard movement. A man yelled, "There's a live one!" just like before. The man took my hand into his. He said, "Just keep on praying," then he called out to others and soon I could hear them discussing the situation and planning the best way to get me out. The man asked me my name. Once again, I took a deep breath and hollered it out. After three tries, he understood: "Priscilla." When he asked my last name I refused to answer. I was worn out. All I could think was, "Forget my name. Just keep digging!"

They weren't sure how to get me out, and the more they discussed it, the more frightened I became. They brought in some chains and the "jaws of life." From time to time I could hear someone ask the man holding my hand if I was alert. Each time I would squeeze his hand as a signal and he would pass it on. After a while another man took my hand. Eventually they were able to relieve some of the pressure on my head. It was then I heard a woman crying out for help. It was the first time I'd heard another victim near me.

They were able to free my right arm, then began working on my legs. The pain was excruciating as I was forced to scrape my legs across the jagged cement in order to free them up. Next they worked on the slab pinning my head. They explained that they would need to flip me out of there quickly as soon as they had the space. It was obvious they were concerned that any movement at all could cause dangerous shifts in the tons of concrete all around.

When the moment finally came, they flipped me over onto my back. I looked straight up and could see the sky. When I turned my head to the left, the sight was horrifying. I could see the extent of destruction and dozens of rescuers climbing all over the place. I also started feeling a great deal of pain. Each breath sent sharp blades stabbing through my chest. As difficult as it was just to breathe, I couldn't help but think of my friends as I looked up and could see straight through the building. I was rushed to St. Anthony Hospital, where I was treated for broken ribs, a collapsed lung, and lacerations. Scrapes and bruises covered me from one end to the other. A friend observed that I looked as though I'd been beaten up with a baseball bat.

My family, meanwhile, had been living a nightmare, not expecting to see me alive again. My son, Jason, and friend Brenda Hatfield were already at St. Anthony, waiting for my name to show up on the list of the dead. It was 2:00 P.M. before they knew I was alive. That evening, a nurse told me a fireman had called to check on me. He was the one who had held my hand and then left for tools. Later, I learned that it was the second bomb scare that had forced the men to leave. His phone call was all it took for me to forgive, and I was thankful they had chosen not to reveal the part about the bomb, as well. A few days later I met the firemen who actually rescued me. They told me I was found about four feet below the first floor. I also met the policeman who had held my hand and told me to keep praying. He told me I had squeezed his hand *hard*. I told him, "I let that first one get away, and I wasn't about to let you go!"

While I was trapped, I had thoughts of sharing my story with all my friends in the building. Sadly, most of my friends died, including Paul and Claude, whose bodies were found several days later. After falling four floors with tons of rubble coming down on me, there simply is no answer to my survival, except that by the grace of God, I was chosen to live.

∽

La Risa Bruner is a survivor of the explosion.

I looked up at the clock, because the credit union opens at 9:00 A.M. and I had received my income tax return.

At that moment I lost my vision and was in total darkness. I sensed something fall, so I covered my head with my arms and slid under my desk. I couldn't get any air. It seemed

Above: The remains of the debris-filled crater left by the Ryder truck's detonation.   **— Photo courtesy of Oscar Johnson**
Below: The Athenian Restaurant, located opposite the Murrah Building, would have been open for business on April 19.

— Photo courtesy of Oscar Johnson

like forever as I brushed stuff off my head. The next thing I knew, Sergeant Solera was under the desk, telling me to get out. He said it was a bomb. He could tell by the way the air smelled. He told me he was hurt really bad, but we had to get out of the building in case another one went off.

I stood up and looked around, still in a daze. Wires were hanging down from the ceiling. I walked to what I thought was the window and was going to jump down when a man grabbed me by the arm and said, "The stairs are over here." I don't know who that man was, but I think he had on a white shirt. I called to Sergeant Solera, who was bleeding badly from his legs. We helped each other to the stairs and outside. When we got out to the benches, we sat down and took his belt and wrapped it around his legs to try to slow the bleeding.

We sat holding each other and looking at the south side of the building, not really knowing what had happened or the fact that a lot of our friends weren't going to come out. An ambulance arrived, and I helped Solera to the street, where they put him on a stretcher. I held his hand and told him he would be just fine. He kept telling me his back was burning. We didn't know it yet, but his back was full of glass from the windows.

As they took him away, more people came out. I began to look for my people. I saw Captain Martin sitting all by himself, and I went over to him. Someone had put a tourniquet on his arms, and his lap was full of blood. His head was also covered with blood. He wouldn't talk to me, so I rubbed his shoulder and talked to him. Finally, he began to answer me. I saw a few more people from the Battalion before the medics took me to the hospital.

∞

Jessie Flint was on her way to the Social Security Office at the Murrah Building with her granddaughter when the bomb detonated.

111

On the way there I had to exit at 10th Street and double back to 13th to get gas. Had I not done this, I would have been right in front of the building.

Moments later, as I went through the intersection at 6th and Robinson, the blast blew the glass out of the side of my car. I was about half a minute away. The police sent me to St. Anthony Hospital, where we called my son, and he came right down.

They started bringing in all the bleeding children and other injured. I told the nurse that I would go to my family doctor because these people needed them more than I did.

They released me. My doctor picked shards of glass out of my face and neck.

∽

Maurice M. Darnell, 85, lives with his wife at the Regency Tower, located across the intersection from the Murrah Building. He wrote an account of his experiences on April 19 for the **Webster County Citizen** *in Missouri, a newspaper for which he served as publisher from 1940 to 1949.*

I was in the elevator ascending to my office when the big boom came. The building shook, and my first thought was that one of the elevators had dropped. I immediately returned to street level only to find the streets and sidewalks covered with broken glass from nearly every building in the area. Black smoke was blowing from the north, so I started walking as fast as I could with my cane. I learned the location of the trouble, but the police would not let me enter certain streets. Finally, I told a policeman my wife was on the fifteenth floor of the Regency Tower and was sick.

I found my wife, Smillka, sitting calmly in the lobby, wearing only a nightgown and a light robe. She was covered with a blanket provided by a kindly Red Cross lady. Smillka's face, scalp, and legs were covered with dried blood, but for me, at that moment, she was the most beautiful woman in Oklahoma.

Fortunately, she had been in our living room instead of one of the bedrooms, which were on the side nearest the Federal Building. She had been showered with broken glass, and we later learned that every window in the twenty-four-story building had been blown out.

After a few minutes in the lobby, everyone was ordered out because of fear of another bomb. We moved out farther west on 5th Street and got Smillka seated on the curb. My son, Dick, found us there and took us to Presbyterian Hospital.

Smillka and I were both exhausted. We had been sick with the flu and colds through March and were just getting our strength back. Thankfully, our Regency landlord is providing food and shelter. All we need now is to regain our strength.

$$\infty$$

Barbara Hays, computer operator for the C.R. Anthony Company, was near the delivery dock at the time of the nearby blast.

I was about three steps from the stairs that go down to the garage doors when I heard a noise and looked up. The doors were exploding in. I first thought someone had run into the doors. I couldn't take my eyes off those doors. All at once glass and everything started flying around me.

Something hit me and I fell to the floor with my hands above my head. I landed between some cases of computer paper. I must have blacked out, because the next thing I remember a man was helping me up and asking if I was all right. I said I was, but when I looked at my hands there was blood all over them.

I was bleeding so much I couldn't tell where it was coming from. A lady showed up, a nurse just getting off work.

She checked me and another injured worker and told a nearby policeman we were going into shock and needed an ambulance. He said he'd see what he could do, but it was "a hell of a mess all over here."

The nurse told me her van was outside and, after breaking out more glass, they passed us through the window opening and into her van. I don't remember much except thinking I was going to bleed all over her seats. At the hospital I saw so many badly hurt people. Then I saw a baby and almost went crazy right there.

I kept telling the doctors it was only a scratch. But the cut was deep and still bleeding, so they set up an IV and another doctor ordered an X-ray to make sure the cut hadn't gone through my chest. After they sewed me up I was released. When my husband got there we hugged for a while, then walked out. We must have looked awful because people kept asking if we were okay. I had lost my heels somewhere. It wasn't until we tried to get back to the building to get my purse that I found out what had happened.

Later at home, I found a large cut on the left side of my head. A doctor cleaned it up the next day, but I still have headaches.

∽

Teri Round is an oncology nurse at Presbyterian Hospital.

The hospital rocked back and forth with the sound. Heads popped out of patient rooms in puzzlement, as I walked down the hall. A crowd stood up in unison at the nurses station and walked to the window, as physicians and nursing staff looked for an answer. One doctor said tensely, "Find out what that was," as I picked up the phone to call Engineering. He later told me the sound reminded him of being in Vietnam when a mortar went off nearby.

I made my way down the stairs from the 7th floor to the staffing office to get my assignment. I went to our Eye Sur-

Above: The parking lot on 5th Street hours after the bombing.
— **Photo courtesy of Penny Turpen James**

A panoramic view of the devastated Alfred P. Murrah Building.
— **Photo courtesy of David Allen**

gery Center, which was now Shock/Burn, and saw a mixture of normal eye surgery cases with their families and a woman who was dressed in a silk blouse and slacks. Her pearls were in place, but her face was covered in blood. A few pieces of glass stuck out of her skin and the look on her face was hard to describe. Bewildered? Shocked? Unable to comprehend? She sat silently in the wheelchair as I began to clean her face.

Ophthalmologists, their surgeries interrupted, began to appear. We took the woman to a cubicle to lie down for examination, as the ophthalmologists became trauma doctors. More people, covered with blood and some with holes where they should not be, appeared on stretchers and in wheelchairs until our cubicles were full. Parts of the floor crunched with the glass dragged in with them. Their faces all bore the same dazed look.

∽

Charlie J. Younger is the programs division manager for the Oklahoma Department of Transportation. He was in a meeting on the fourth floor of the Murrah Building at the time of the explosion.

My first reaction was to close my eyes. I felt myself moving and something hit my chest. I landed on my hands and knees against the south wall of the office. When I opened my eyes, there was a deafening roar of wind and I could feel debris hitting the back of my head.

Suddenly, this incredible force changed directions as the collapsing floors and suction created by the implosion blew debris back over us. I felt pain in the back of my head and assumed I'd been smacked by broken glass. As it turned out, small particles of gravel and concrete had imbedded themselves in my scalp.

The entire incident lasted only seconds.

When we stood, I remember looking out an empty window. The windows of the courthouse to the south were broken, too, as if something had been thrown against each one.

Then I looked north to see that the entire front of the building was gone.

We were joined by Jim Erickson, who had been sitting in an adjacent office. We soon realized that Lind was missing. We found him beneath a mass of metal ductwork near the corner of his desk and pulled him free.

We also found and freed another co-worker from debris near where the bomb had shorn away most of the fourth floor. Lind's office was destroyed, but two-thirds of the floor remained intact.

At Erickson's suggestion, we moved to his office. As we did, a series of small explosions punctuated the air — the result of exploding gas tanks in vehicles parked just north of the building.

The interior walls of Erickson's office had disintegrated. Only insulation remained.

I put my hand on the east office wall. It went completely through. I could see approaching fire trucks through the hole. To the north, smoke drifted back into the exposed interior of the building, inching closer to us as the wind shifted. We became concerned over the danger of smoke inhalation.

About twenty minutes later, we saw volunteers removing bodies from the rubble. We decided we'd better start figuring how to get off the floor. A couple of us tried to attract the attention of people in the plaza immediately to the south, while others began making a rope from the tattered remnants of curtains that once framed Erickson's windows.

Finally, we caught the attention of a spectator and told him to get a ladder from a fire truck parked on Robinson. It wasn't long until we heard the sound of the ladder hitting the side of the structure. A sloped six-foot ledge ran along the outside of Erickson's office, blocking our view of the rescuers. As it turned out, the ladder was too short.

An OG&E employee, Rudy Jiminez, arrived in his company pickup, which also had a ladder. It, too, was far short of reaching the fourth floor. We heard someone at ground level suggest stacking debris high enough to allow the ladder to reach us. Soon the red tips of the ladder were seen at the rim of the ledge, followed by a firefighter's helmet.

Gripping the window sill, I edged out onto the ledge, extended my hand, and pulled a rescuer into Lind's office.

Because of the ledge's steep incline, we realized it would be a difficult escape route. Compounding the problem was the fact that the ladder's short length meant rescuers had placed it almost vertically.

Using the curtains as a safety line, I carefully crawled out on the ledge, brushing broken glass out of the way as I went. As I reached the tip of the ladder, others followed, each backing gingerly out the window of Lind's former office.

∞

Kay Keylon is a registered nurse in eye surgery at Presbyterian Hospital.

The injured were covered with lacerations and blood, yet none worried about themselves. They were worried about co-workers, and they wanted their families to know they were okay. We drew strength from them.

We gathered supplies as doctors sutured their wounds. One of my patients had three surgeons suturing her simultaneously. After our patients were stabilized, they were sent for further evaluation or to surgery. We had successfully treated the first "wave." Then came the horrifying news: there would be no more patients. The rest of the victims had not survived the blast. As helpers in this chosen profession, we were suddenly overcome with helplessness. I was okay emotionally — until I left work.

∞

Sue Crosthwait works for Housing and Urban Development.

I had just left my office and gone up to the ninth floor for a computer class. I sat down in the back of the room, and about a minute later the explosion shook the building. Things were falling in on us, and the building was shaking so hard I didn't think any of us would make it out alive. I didn't know it, but the building was collapsing only a few feet away from us. Something hit me in the head and knocked me out of my chair. I remember crawling under a desk for protection, thinking an earthquake had somehow caused it all, though Oklahoma isn't known for its earthquakes.

A co-worker, Robert Roddy, was yelling at me to take his hand. He pulled me out from under the desk and we listened to people yelling at the front of the room as we made our way through the darkness and smoke. There were all kinds of obstacles in our way and we had to climb over a door that had been blown off and was blocking our passage. I remember seeing blood in the stairwell when we got there and wondering, "Where's all the people? Why, with such a terrible thing happening, are there so few people in the stairwell?"

∽

Teresa and Jim Harmon's son, Ian, was in the YMCA daycare center.

My co-workers and I were sitting in the office when we felt a tremor. A few minutes later we were told that the Federal Building had been bombed. We turned on the office TV as the first reports were broadcast. My husband Jim called to tell me what was going on, and I asked him if he realized that the building was on the same block as Ian's daycare. He wasn't aware it was that close.

Jim headed downtown. Once there, he was told by YMCA officials that Ian had been cut on his head and taken to Children's Hospital. In the meantime, my mother, who works downtown, called to tell me she was okay. She then left her office with a friend and started walking toward the

Above: This spontaneous bomb site memorial expanded daily throughout the search and rescue operation.
— **Photo courtesy of Oscar Johnson**

Below: Southward view of the Oklahoma City skyline from 8th Street and Harvey.
— **Photo courtesy of David Allen**

YMCA in search of Ian. When they got close they were stopped by the police. Unable to get through, she decided to go home.

Jim and I checked Children's and then VA hospital with no luck. Finally, we were directed to the Red Cross office. There we found the director of the YMCA daycare. She informed us that Ian had been taken to St. Anthony with a cut on his forehead and a possible concussion. She assured us he would be fine. When we got to the hospital, almost four hours after the bomb exploded, there was Ian, eating graham crackers and flirting with a room full of nurses.

He was kept overnight as a precaution, but doesn't have any obvious lasting injuries. Loud noises seem to bother him, but he doesn't appear to remember anything else.

∞

Barbara Hernandez works only a few blocks from the YMCA, where her daughter, Sarah, was dropped off the morning of April 19.

When we felt the blast it was so strong that we were sure something had happened in our own building. But when I saw the huge cloud of smoke coming from the Federal Building I immediately tried to call the YMCA. No response. No ring, no busy signal, just silence — silence that quickly turned to fear.

Fear gave way to terror as I made my way to the lobby and saw the streets covered with glass. I began running toward the YMCA and was close to hysteria by the time I got there. The air was thick with smoke and injured people were all around. It was bizarre — so many starched white shirts with blood all over them. The contrast was unforgettable. The YMCA had been evacuated. Steel doors were bent and blown from their frames and there wasn't one window left in the room where my daughter would have been only minutes before.

Seconds seemed like hours as I searched frantically for

my baby. Then I learned that triage for the YMCA children had been set up in a nearby parking lot. When I got there, I spotted Sarah being held snugly by a strange man. Both of them looked dazed and were smeared with blood. I took her in my arms, feeling the hysteria replaced by relief. I began the journey back toward my office, clutching her tightly. On the way I was met by another mother from my office running in the direction of the horror I had just left. Her son attended the daycare in the Federal Building. I suspected, sadly, that she would not be as fortunate as I had been. Suddenly, my relief turned to grief as the enormity of the disaster swept over me. I found out later, however, that the woman's son was one of the lucky who was rescued.

Sarah had thirteen minor cuts and a perforated eardrum. She has trouble sleeping and is scared by loud noises, but these are problems we are thankful to have to deal with.

ભ

Clark Peterson is the sole survivor of the four-person Advertising and Public Affairs Office, located on the fourth floor with the U.S. Army Recruiting Battalion.

About 8:58 A.M. I sat three feet from the north windows, as my supervisor gave me final instructions for a project. A few minutes later an electric spark appeared by my computer and everything turned black. Propelled objects raced through the darkness amidst the sound of moaning steel.

I caught a glimpse of a terrified girl with both arms straight up in the air. Both of us were apparently falling, but I didn't realize what had happened until a minute later. The sight of her was so brief and faint that I could not identify her. She yelled, "Ah!" as if there was not enough time to inhale.

At first I thought contact with an electric outlet was causing me to black out, but in a second I knew that was impossible. I was puzzled. Everything changed to a dead-like settling within the black atmosphere. I kept thinking, "What is this?"

As the blackness and dust cleared, I discovered that the armchair I had been seated in had been replaced. I was still in a sitting position, but on ceiling material which turned out to be the top of a three-story pile of collapsed flooring.

∞

Captain Henderson Baker was stationed with the U.S. Army Recruiting Battalion on the Murrah Building's fourth floor.

It probably took five seconds to fall from the fourth to the first floor. It felt like thirty minutes, because of all the things that went through my mind. When I hit the floor, I was dazed but managed to get up. In the midst of the darkness, through dust and smoke, I saw a ray of sunlight shining through and simply followed it out to the street.

∞

Wanda Dalto is a claims representative for the Social Security Administration. She was at work on the first floor of the Murrah Building.

I heard an earth-shattering noise and crawled under my desk. Everything was falling and it was as dark as midnight. Almost as quickly as it began, it stopped — silence at first, then crying and pleas for help. The smell was awful and I felt like I was breathing sand. I couldn't move. I was paralyzed with fear, yet I knew I had to get out quick if I wanted to survive.

I shoved everything out of the way and got out from under the desk. I called out to a co-worker, then crawled toward him over ceiling tiles and an overturned copy machine. I felt for a hand in the darkness, as he reached out to me. We hugged for a moment, trying to make sense of what had just happened. As the dust thinned, a small ray of light began to show under our break room door. The outside door had to be open, so we followed the light until we reached it. There, another co-worker appeared. Her face was covered with blood, but she was able to walk. The three of us escaped together.

Outside, helicopters were flying overhead and sirens were screaming. I thought all of downtown had been bombed. Some officials directed us to head for the Myriad Convention Center, so I walked those few blocks, wondering how I would be able to contact my family. I was standing with a large group of people across the street from the Myriad when I gazed out over the crowd and saw the tear-stained but smiling face of my husband. He had come to rescue me.

∽

Jack Gobin was at his desk in the U.S. Department of Agriculture offices on the fifth floor at 9:02 a.m.

A rumbling sound, violent shaking, and loss of lights occurred at the same instant. I remember glancing over my left shoulder toward the south wall of windows at my back and seeing the venetian blinds moving. The time must have been measured in milliseconds, but it was enough to decide that we were having an earthquake and I needed to get under my desk. Then the windows imploded, and I was blasted with glass that cut the back of my arms and imbedded itself in the back of my head. My next memory is that of climbing out from under my desk, which was still in place. I may have passed out briefly; the phone receiver was still in my hand. My room was demolished, but somehow I missed seeing it happen. There was no more shaking or rumbling, and my thoughts turned to the possibility of a tornado. Then the gas tanks of the burning cars began to explode, and I decided

Above:
One of several
memorial services
held in front of
the remains of the
Federal Building.
— **Photo courtesy of
David Allen**

Right:
An isolated flag
atop a surviving
column stands as a
symbol of survival.
— **Photo courtesy of
David Allen**

that we were under enemy air attack and must have received a direct bomb hit.

Nothing seemed real. It was like a dream. The devastation I was seeing could not be. My secretary, Cindy King, started screaming my name, and I called back. Through a pile of collapsed walls I saw another colleague, Dr. Brian Espe, emerging. I knew we could not all be having the same bad dream. We asked each other, "What happened?" What seemed like a nightmare slowly began to sink in as reality.

Black smoke rolled into the building from the burning cars across the street, and I had momentary fear of the building burning. The smoke density varied with the wind, and it became evident that the fire was north of the building. With the ceiling and walls gone I realized there wasn't much left to burn anyway.

∽

Registered Nurse Rita Cink works in the emergency room at Presbyterian Hospital.

The victims were triaged by doctors in front of our emergency entrance. Walking wounded and wheelchair patients were sent down the hall to a smaller M*A*S*H unit, set-up in the eye surgery and outpatient surgery department. Stretcher victims were brought into the ER, where every cubicle was set up as a trauma room. When victims were wheeled into the ER, someone would yell, "Nurse, we have a neuro!" and the neuro doctors and nurses would hit that room. Some victims were wheeled directly to surgery without stopping in ER to get stabilized. The triage doctors would say, "We need the surgeons for this one," and the surgeons would take the patient on the stretcher up the elevator to OR.

We had runners that literally ran wherever they needed to go. One runner even ran to Children's Hospital to borrow some special needles we needed for our "pedi's." Children's never questioned the request and handed them right to our runner. Dietary brought food, drinks, and snacks to support the enormous outpouring of staff that worked all day. They kept everything stacked up, so no one even had to ask. It was all so impressive from the medical viewpoint, and I felt honored to be a part of the team.

By mid-afternoon we had stopped getting patients. Everyone disbanded and we started putting away supplies and trying to return the emergency room to normal. Transport was cleaning stretchers and bringing them back to ER. One of the transport workers found a pair of little white tennis shoes and, not quite sure what to do with them, handed them to me. It nearly broke my heart. One lonely, wet pair of tennis shoes and we couldn't even identify the little owner. Forever engraved in my mind are those tiny white tennis shoes.

∽

Linda Logan is a survivor of the Murrah Building's Social Security Office.

In the twinkling of an eye, life as we knew it was no more. As I stood in front of the manager's desk there was a black flash. The next conscious moment found me flat on my back in about two inches of water, covered with debris. As I struggled to free myself, I could hear nothing. Thinking I was alone, I realized I had to get up before I drowned in the rising water.

I yelled for help and shoved on the heavy object pinning me to the floor. After what seemed a long time, I heard the manager say, "Linda, I'm trying to get to you." Hearing that voice seemed to give me strength and I gave another shove, freeing my upper body. I was then able to pull myself completely loose. As I felt around the floor, trying to find my glasses, Gwen Greaves, who had just been freed from her chair, grabbed my wrist. I heard Eric McKisick say, "Come this way. I think I can see some light." We crawled over file cabinets and dodged hanging wires as we followed his voice to the light, out the door, and up the steps to Robinson Street.

In a shocked stupor I began to search for my best friend, Wanda, asking everyone I knew if they'd seen her. It would be late afternoon before I knew she was safe. I heard people talking about a bomb. Surely not, I thought.

Wet cold, and confused, I waited to be transported to Bethany Hospital. After X-rays and an exam, my husband and I went home to begin a very painful healing.

∞

Dr. John Beavers was one-year-old Baylee Almon's pediatrician.

About an hour after the explosion, I saw Aren Almon in the hallway at the hospital. She found me and told me that Baylee had been in the daycare center in the building and asked if I would please help find her. I inquired with St. Anthony and then called Children's Hospital, where many of the children involved in the bombing were taken. No one fitting Baylee's description had been brought to their emergency rooms. Shortly thereafter, I got news that a young female child was brought to St. Anthony Hospital and was dead on arrival. I went to the morgue and viewed the body of a baby girl, lifeless and covered with dust and dirt. The child's head was wrapped in gauze, due most likely to a head injury. At first I did not recognize the child as Baylee. Maybe it was her altered appearance, or perhaps it was just my subconscious not allowing me to see this child as the patient I had known and cared for. I left the morgue and then returned with my office manager. Together we took a closer look at the innocent child who lay lifeless on the table. At that point we both knew this was Baylee and that she was gone.

In the number of years I have practiced medicine I have had to deal with death on several occasions, both with the patient and patient's family. Although it is never easy to talk about death, it is certainly more understandable when it is secondary to a terminal disease or an accident. When death involves an innocent child such as Baylee and is caused by a senseless act of terrorism, words cannot describe the sorrow that fills your heart. In all my years of medicine, telling Aren Almon that Baylee was dead was the hardest and saddest thing I have ever had to do. I can't even imagine the torment that went through Aren in those moments.

I saw Baylee for the last time on April 19, 1995. On April 21 she was on the front page of the local newspaper and nearly every other paper in the free world. The photograph of the fireman holding Baylee's lifeless body quickly became a symbol of the innocence lost and the senselessness of this terrorist act. With that picture, Baylee's death touched the hearts of men and women all over the world, just as her life had touched the hearts of all of us at Saints Pediatric Associates. Of the millions of people who have seen Baylee's picture, we consider ourselves blessed to have shared a small portion of her life. We were among the lucky few who had seen her smiling face and heard her laughter ring through our hallways. Every medical practice has a patient that no one will ever forget. I can truly say that none of us here will ever forget Baylee Almon. We mourn her death, but we celebrate and rejoice in the life she shared with us.

∽

Germaine Johnston is Chief of Multi-family Asset Management for HUD. She lost thirty-five co-workers in the blast.

Just as Don Bewley and I started talking, the ceiling fell in. After that we couldn't see each other, but I said, "My God, Don, what is happening to us?" I did not hear the bomb explode, but I heard people screaming — not words, just screams. Many, many screams. I heard popping noises, which I later realized were the sounds of the concrete floors snapping in two. Then I heard a roar and more popping sounds, as the floors collapsed on top of each other. I heard

Above: Sharlotte Campbell and her monkey "Charlie."
— **Photo courtesy of Sharlotte Campbell**

Below: Pete Gutzmann and Jeff Zentzis of White Bear Lake, Minnesota.
— **Photo courtesy of Jeff Zentzis**

the noise of glass and other debris raining down on top of the ceiling tile that now covered and protected me from the onslaught of flying concrete and granite. It was a miracle that nothing heavy landed on top of me.

I have no sense of the time that elapsed before the sounds and the shower of debris stopped. It seemed like an eternity, though most likely it was only two or three minutes. When it stopped, I could hear the cars across the street exploding and burning. Don was still sitting in front of my desk. We pushed the ceiling tiles, sprinkler pipes, duct work, and wires off of us and tried to decide what had happened. I thought an airplane had collided with the building. Don thought it might be a natural gas explosion. But as the smoke and dust began to clear, we realized how much of the building was gone. We could see all the way to the ground, and we could see the sky, and we could see those cars burning across the street.

Don finally said, "Germaine, I think it was a bomb, and I think you and I are lucky people." He was bleeding profusely from a gash on top of his head. It was about then that I realized there was no floor two feet to my left and two feet behind me. In fact, both my bookcase and my credenza were gone. We realized we were sitting on a tiny platform held up by one of the building's twenty-eight-inch support columns.

∞

Ivan Wisley works for Housing and Urban Development. He was in the men's restroom on the eighth floor when the bomb detonated.

I was struck by parts of both the ceiling and a wall, knocking me to the floor. It was instantly dark and the room filled with dust. I managed to reach the door, and once in the hallway I found a fellow employee bleeding severely. I got to her, and after we made it to the stairwell, we moved carefully down the stairs. Visibility was poor.

At the seventh floor we met two other employees. It seemed like forever before we reached the door to the outside. People were running everywhere. A policeman directed me to take the injured woman to the street, where emergency teams were treating wounded. I stayed with her until they dressed her wounds and she was taken to the hospital.

After the second bomb scare, I managed to get a ride home with a complete stranger who seemed concerned about me in view of the blood on my clothes and shoes. Actually, I had received only a bruised leg and a bump on the head.

With time I'm sure this nightmare will disappear, even though we lost most of the people in my division. I've had trouble sleeping.

ϖ

Lorri McNiven was at work in the Social Security Office on the first floor at 9:02 A.M.

My desk was located on the bottom floor midway between the front and back part of the Social Security Office. I felt pressure and vibration—I really don't know how to explain it. If I heard the bomb, it was like in a tunnel. It seemed far away. I remember a sensation like falling, then thinking I was dying, that I had suffered an aneurysm or a stroke or maybe I had electrocuted myself from having my hands on my computer. I also remember hearing a male voice saying, "What's happening, what's happening?" I believe I then lost consciousness for possibly half an hour or more.

When I came to, I heard all the noise. I heard voices begging for help. I remember thinking that the voices were crying for help for me. I didn't realize at that point that the whole office had been affected. I was still thinking it was my own private hell, that people were calling for help for me because of the "heart attack" or whatever I had suffered. It took me only a short period to realize I was not badly hurt, and that I was in total darkness. Cold water was pouring on me, which convinced me that I needed to move. Because of the darkness, I couldn't determine what I was lying on. I didn't know until later that the blast had blown my contacts out of my eyes. I felt around. All I could feel was metal edges, jagged cement, glass and grit. I noticed a blur of light above me and wanted to get to it. I didn't know at the time that the light was a crack in the building.

I crawled up toward the light. I was pulling up on computer cable wires and thinking if I hadn't already electrocuted myself, I was going to do so now for sure. I climbed up as far as I could, then couldn't go any farther, as I was too big to fit through the cracks in the concrete. By now I realized I had no contacts in my eyes, yet could see through the crack that there was a lot of smoke billowing. I looked at my watch. It was 9:40. A little while after that I noticed flashlights around the perimeter of an area I could look down at. I started waving my arms and asking if anyone could see me. All around me others were calling for help and crying out as well.

∞

Dennis Purifoy works for the Social Security Administration as an assistant district manager.

I saw a yellow flash and was knocked out of my chair. Everything went pitch black and stuff fell on my head. I thought maybe the computer had blown up, but that didn't account for the darkness. I wasn't sure if I could see. I started trying to move the stuff covering me. It was like being in a collapsed tent, and I couldn't move the web of junk draped over me. I think I was sitting on my rear.

I yelled for help over and over. Finally, I heard another voice close by. It was Dan DeMoss. He said, "I hear you," I yelled back, "Where are you? I can't see anything." He replied, "Look. Here's my hand," and he poked his hand

133

through the clutter. I saw it, grabbed it, and he was able to help me get up.

We were dazed and incredulous, trying to figure out what happened. We saw some light to our left and moved toward it. All the walls, except some concrete ones, had been blown away, and water could be heard running from broken pipes. We saw an injured employee, barely alive and in shock, or so it appeared. I'll never forget how she looked, and it was then we realized how bad the damage was. We knew we had to find a way out.

We climbed up a pile of broken walls. We heard voices calling from the supply room farther back from the skylight, which was the source of the light we'd been trying to reach. We went over and helped them climb the pile, too. Tillie, Liz, and Gina were all okay. We had to crouch under a concrete ledge at the edge of the skylight to avoid falling objects. We saw John Cresswell and another GSA employee on the second floor. Dan and I yelled, "Turn off the water! Turn off the water!"

Dan and I went back to try to move the injured lady to the skylight, where we hoped rescuers could get her out. But we were able to move her only a short distance because of the destruction. It was very frustrating. We felt helpless, not being able to help her. I left her with Dan and headed back to the area we had come from originally, hoping to get a flashlight from my own office. Unfortunately, I couldn't even locate the file cabinet it was in, so I walked on, shouting, "Can anybody hear me?" I got no response. I continued calling out, walking, and looking.

Finally, someone heard my call and answered. I said, "Where are you?" She replied, "I don't know. I can't see!" I yelled back, "I can't see, either. Keep talking so I can find you." We talked back and forth until I found her. It was Lorri McNiven. I could see her only because of a little patch of light behind her. I moved some junk out of the way so she wouldn't get cut. She was barefooted, having been blown out of her shoes. I helped her down and led her toward the back doors, stepping carefully.

When we got to the back, firemen started coming in.

Left: Surrounded by the Federal Building's rubble, a lone chair sits awkwardly upright.
— **Photo courtesy of Oscar Johnson**

Below: Red roses lie scattered amid the Federal Building's debris in memory of the bombing's 169 victims.
— **Photo courtesy of David Allen**

The door and a twisted door frame were moved out of the way. We walked outside and into the bright sun. I ran around to the south side and up to the skylight, which is at ground level there. A policeman stopped me and said I couldn't go back in. I tried to explain about the people inside, and for the first time started crying. After he left, I went to the skylight, only to find they had all been taken out by a ladder. I tried once more to get back through the police lines to show them where to look, but they wouldn't let me.

An EMT put some gauze on my bleeding ear. Someone was going around offering drinks of water. Water never tasted better. We evacuated farther away, and I used the phone at Safelite Auto Glass to call my wife, Cassie. I went from there to the Oklahoma City Clinic to get stitched. It was there that Cassie picked me up.

I still don't know the "why" and may never know, but I do know that evil didn't triumph totally. And I know something else: we showed what real Americans are made of that day.

cos

Robyn Parent is an employee of HUD, which was located on the seventh floor of the Murrah Building.

I was admitted to the hospital and when I was put in my room that afternoon I saw the north side of the building for the first time on television. I could not believe it. I totally lost it. The nurse had to sedate me to calm me down. I don't know how anyone got out of the building. I was released from the hospital on Friday, April 21, my 35th birthday. I had a concussion of the optic nerve and a torn and detached retina to my left eye. I also had a cut on my left arm, lots of bruises and fragments of glass all over me.

cos

Registered Nurse Linda Sanders was on duty at University Hospital. Her father, James Carver, was on the fourth floor of the Federal Building.

That Wednesday I was Charge Nurse in the Cardiovascular Intensive Care Unit. After the explosion, I received a call from my Head Nurse to implement the disaster plan. My first duty was to clear the unit of all stable patients. I started notifying physicians of patient transfers and preparing patients to be moved.

At one point I stopped to watch the news on TV. The reporter kept saying the Courthouse had been bombed. My heart sank, as I realized the building on the TV was not the Courthouse but the Federal Building — where my father, James Carver, worked. I grabbed the phone and started frantically dialing my father's office. It rang and rang, but no one answered. My eyes filled with tears. I realized that no one was going to answer. I felt numb.

I tried calling RNs on the disaster plan, but the lines were jammed. I began to work feverishly, moving patients out, cleaning and stocking rooms, making sure the right equipment was at hand. All the while I was fighting the panic I felt inside.

Finally, a co-worker called in from outside. I gave her a list of RNs numbers to call, as well as my mother's number. "Tell her to find Dad," I said.

The unit was quiet except for TV news reports. We waited for the patients we were sure to get. My hands were shaking. I had to get busy, so I went to ER to help.

The ER was a mass of nurses, doctors, and techs. I knew many of them. I grabbed someone and told him I needed to keep busy, because my dad was in that building. He just looked at me with a blank expression.

I stocked trauma rooms, replaced equipment, and helped other nurses with patients. It kept coming out of my mouth to people I knew, "My dad's office is in that building." I kept getting the same blank looks from them.

At some point my mother called and left word that she hadn't been able to locate Dad, either. Images of him flashed through my mind: his grin, his voice, his stance. It startled me, and I realized I had been searching the faces of victims coming into ER. I was searching for my dad.

A few hours later I talked to my mom again. My dad had survived. She was on her way to pick him up. Tears ran down my face, and I began shaking all over. I looked at my co-workers. There were these blank stares again. I smiled, so they would know. For the first time that day they laughed. Their support was indescribable. The Cardiology PA told me, "Go hug your dad for us."

By the time I got to my parents' house, my dad was there—scratched, bruised, dusty, and grinning.

His office was on the fourth floor. Most of it was gone. He had been at his desk, talking on the phone, when the bomb went off. He was thrown against the wall behind him and remembers thinking as he flew backwards, "That damn computer blew up!"

He soon realized he was on a four-foot ledge, which was all that was left of his office. Family pictures were lying at his side. He picked them up, along with a jacket my mother had given him, and called out to see if anyone was around him. No one answered. About an hour later he was rescued from the ledge. The fireman asked him to leave the pictures, so his hands would be free to climb down the ladder. "Nope. Not gonna do it," he said.

After Dad got down from the ledge, a physician bandaged his hands. Not knowing what else to do, Dad embraced the pictures and started walking north on Robinson, toward home.

∽

James Carver worked on the fourth floor of the Murrah Building for the Federal Highway Administration. Eleven of his fifteen co-workers died in the blast.

The explosion blew me against the wall of my office. I

thought my computer had blown up. I felt a sharp pain in my side, and I remember thinking it would be a good idea to check myself for injuries as soon as I had time. I wound up sitting on the floor with my back against the west wall. Pieces of desk, wallboard, wire and duct work were piled everywhere, including on top of me.

I heard moans and groans and pieces of building still falling from the upper floors. I purposely sat there for a time, moving my legs and arms to see if everything was working and to make sure I wasn't bleeding so badly it was dangerous. I was sitting on a ledge, and I could see over the edge all the way down to the pile of broken floors below. I saw the cars across the street burning, and I could see the wide open sky. Then I noticed how small the ledge was where I saw — WOW! A couple more feet and I would've been gone.

I decided to sit very still. Sometime later, when I was confident the ledge was going to hold, I cleared the junk off me and started to stand up. That's when I noticed the pictures of my children and their families lying on the floor beside me. I picked them up, knowing if I didn't I would never see them again. I climbed over about six feet of stuff, toward the front of the building, and shouted something like, "Is anyone there? Does anyone need help?" I got no response, so I waited, then tried again. Still no response. I kept moving toward the window. My hands were bleeding, but not badly enough to worry about. I finally got to the window and stood up in the sill. Down below, I could see people scurrying about all over the place.

A fireman shouted up and asked if I was all right. I yelled back that I was and made the A-OK sign. I told him to take care of those who were hurt first. He shouted back that if I got dizzy, to sit down. I felt pretty safe there on the window sill. After what seemed like a long time, I saw the firemen put a ladder up to a nearby window. They called up to me and asked if I could move over to where they were. I knew I couldn't, and let them know. They told me to stay put.

After a while, the firemen moved the ladder over to my window. The sill outside had a steep slant on it. One of the

Above: Painted Xs on the front of the Oklahoma Water Resources Board Building identify pockmarks from flying debris.

— Photo courtesy of Hal McKnight

Below: Clutter from the Oklahoma Water Resources Board Building blocks Harvey just north of 5th Street.

— Photo courtesy of Hal McKnight

firemen climbed to the end of the ladder, then held onto the metal frame of the window and told me to climb down *him* until I reached the ladder, which had just barely reached the slanted ledge. They let me take all the time I needed. They also asked me to put down the photos so I could use both hands, but I was somewhat stubborn about it; there was no way I was turning loose of those pictures, and I told them so.

On the ground, I was led out to 4th Street, where a doctor bandaged my hands. Not knowing quite what to do, and still dazed, I wandered around for a bit. When the area was evacuated by the threat of another bomb, I decided to go find a phone and call Jeanene, my wife. Still somewhat confused, I started walking north on Harvey until I came to a printing shop, where I called home, only to get no answer. I continued on, and encountered some people in a car who asked me if the explosion was a nuclear device. I said I didn't know. I must have looked a mess, because soon after another stranger stopped me and asked if I wanted to use his mobile phone. This time Jeanene answered. When we got over the shock, we agreed that I would move a block east and continue walking, on Robinson, and she would bring the van to get me. She called the kids, then headed out.

I walked all the way to 23rd Street, then rested there until Jeanene arrived. We had coffee at a nearby fast food place, then went home. It felt so good to be safe at home with some of my family around me. Before I took a shower, I shook the glass and other stuff out of my hair and a surprising amount of glass out of my pockets. I don't know how it got inside my pockets.

∞

Brett Scott Brooks was in his office at the Journal Record Building when the explosion occurred across the street.

The blast blew me out of my chair and brought part of the ceiling and walls tumbling down on my head, back, and hands. When I realized what had happened, I got up and shouted at other employees who were standing around in the aisles. I screamed at them to get out of there. About a dozen of them took off for the exits. The rest were either trapped or injured. I heard Druicillia, who was trapped, cry for help. I got her to safety, then went to the south side of the building to help some of the others.

I managed to look outside and saw the real target had been the Federal Building. There were many fires. I noticed about a dozen or so dead bodies just lying there, and cars totaled by the blast were burning furiously.

∽

Tom Janssen is chief of orthopedic surgery at St. Anthony Hospital, which is about eight blocks from the Murrah Building. He worked in the emergency room all day on April 19.

Anticipating there would be victims coming to the hospital, I changed into surgical scrubs and proceeded to the emergency room. As I was heading down the stairs, I received a page to the ER, followed by 9-1-1. In my professional career, I had never received a 9-1-1 page before. This was a first, and I had little doubt that a true disaster had occurred.

When I arrived at the ER, one of the first patients was already there. She was a young lady who appeared to be in good condition except for a badly broken wrist and hand. She told me she was one of the fortunate people who miraculously walked out of the building. She warned us that we would soon be seeing many seriously injured patients. She was right. They started arriving at a frightening pace, many of them critically hurt.

We had to prioritize treatment of the more serious injuries. Patients who were stable were promptly transported to other units in the hospital. As the Chief of Orthopedic Surgery, I was evaluating all orthopedic injuries, but there were soon more of them than I could take care of myself. I was overwhelmed with the volume of patients flowing into the emergency room. Fortunately, the response by the medical staff was quick, and the situation was soon brought under control.

I will never forget leaving surgery that night. A young couple stood just outside the entrance to surgery. They both had fear on their faces. They had a picture of a family member they were looking for. I wanted so badly to be able to tell them the Jane Doe in surgery was their loved one, but unfortunately this was not the case. I discovered later that their relative was found in the rubble of the building.

I left the hospital to go home around 8:00 P.M. It was difficult to leave. Even though the day had been long, I felt there was much more I needed to be doing. Lifting and bending all day had left me with severe back pain, but it was no greater than the pain in my heart for all the victims I'd seen and their families. I would have gladly stayed through the night, if only there had been more survivors to treat.

∽

Shon Simpson had resigned his job as chief of water quality for the Oklahoma Water Resources Board prior to April 19, but he was still at work that day. He now lives in Arkansas.

The window in front of me turned solid gray as it shattered. An unbelievable violent force lifted me off the ground and threw me back several feet. While I was in the air, time moved extremely slow. I hit the floor face down about five feet from where I had been standing. I knew there had been an explosion and that a lot of glass had hit me in the face.

I became aware of a lot of blood running from my face, down my hands, and onto the floor. I had no idea how badly I was hurt, but I remember being very still and not knowing whether or not I could move — and being scared to try. My first recollection of sound after the blast was of a cry for help from my secretary, Denise Hill, who was about twenty feet away. I heard Juli Watterson say, "Shon needs an ambulance. He's bleeding real bad and not moving."

I thought that we were on fire. My impression while airborne was that a gasoline truck had collided with something and exploded right outside the west windows on Harvey Street. I could smell a burnt odor and assumed that the building had been doused with gas.

After a few seconds, I asked Juli to look around and see if we were burning. She said "no" and went to help Denise, who had been buried under shelves and a filing cabinet. Soon I realized that my hands were getting sticky when I pressed them to my forehead. The bleeding had slowed.

A group of five or six of us climbed through the window that had exploded. There were only a few people milling around. We went to the intersection of 5th and Harvey and looked back east.What I saw looked like a surreal hell. You could not take a step without crunching glass. Thick smoke rolled out of the parking lot up the street. I could see daylight through the Federal Building, and it was clear the front of it was gone. We knew that many, many people were dead.

∞

David Roy is a staff assistant with the Oklahoma State Regents for Higher Education. His office was in the Journal Record Building.

The whole building shook and my throat and lungs burned like they were on fire. The next thing I remember is opening my eyes to utter destruction. The ceiling had collapsed and a light fixture had hit me in the head. My glasses had been blown off and were lying on the desk next to the wall.

I reached out, put my glasses on, then looked around. Part of the roof had crashed down on me. A wall had been

Above: A. J. Haines III and his search dog, Reno.
— **Photo courtesy of A. J. Haines III**

Below: The Reverend Samuel Craig.
— **Photo courtesy of Samuel Craig**

blown into my area, pinning me against my desk. I was able to move the light fixture which, oddly, was still on. I stood up. I had no idea what had happened. I turned around and was able to see through the holes in the walls to where a window used to be. I could see flames and smoke outside. I managed to get enough of the wall pushed away to turn around and fold my wheelchair so I could take it out with me.

As I made my way out of my cubicle I checked for my co-worker, Sheila, in her office, then checked for Jody. I was alone. I then heard someone yelling, "Is there anyone else back there?"

I hollered back, and Rick Sikora stuck his head in. I told him I was the only one left and we started out. Somebody yelled that there was someone hurt in the break room, so I told Rick to go help and I would make it out okay. I walked on, pushing my wheels in front of me until I got to the stairs. At that point Rundell Henderson appeared and helped me and my wheels get down the stairs and out of the building. From there I was able to get back into my chair and start locating my co-workers.

Later that evening, at home, I found pieces of glass in my backpack. It was glass from the Federal Building.

ↄ∞ↄ

Susan Urbach was in her office in the Journal Record Building at 9:02 A.M.

There was this great *"kaboom,"* and I watched the office literally explode in front of me. I saw the suspended ceiling fall. Then the plaster ceiling and the walls came down. I was knocked to the ground on my right side, leaving my left side to take the full force of everything that fell. I remember being covered up, and my first thought was that I just needed to get out of that place. Since my arms were above my head it was very awkward, but I was able to get everything off of me and climb out. I didn't stop to look back, to check anything, or even try to find the shoes that were no longer on

146

my feet. Brian, June, and I headed for the door, walking over several feet of the wreckage that used to be our office. I noticed that the top of my suit was all the way open. I tried to button it on the way out, but found I no longer had any buttons.

I took some pretty good hits. My face was cut up, and my ear was almost cut in two. My left elbow took some jagged and dirty cuts from plaster and concrete, but my back was the worst, having taken a large load of glass. One injury was like a stab wound that went very deep, almost into the chest cavity. Otherwise, I was peppered with it, like from a shotgun blast.

When will life get back to normal? It won't. My old normal does not exist. This is true to some extent for anyone living in Oklahoma City. I am a "downtowner." My life and community revolves there, and much of it had been destroyed forever or severely wounded. I bank at the Federal Employees Credit Union, which was in the Murrah Building. Half the employees were killed and the building is gone. Three of the four people I knew at HUD are dead. My own office was demolished, the building it was in completely gutted. All the people have been dispersed. Nearly every morning I visited the YMCA, which won't open again for at least eighteen months, if ever. I utilized the little post office on 5th Street, which now may be torn down. I used to eat at the Athenian from time to time. That building was destroyed, too. The public library, my personal and business haunt, is closed for an indeterminate time, and its employees have been re-assigned within the system.

From my office window I could see the pretty First United Methodist Church, which now will have to be torn down. Looking the other direction, I could see St. Joseph's Old Cathedral, which still stands bravely but is seriously damaged. Standing tall but limping a little, it continues to serve its mission as a presence in downtown Oklahoma City. Our flock gathers round, concretely realizing that indeed the church is not just a building. Even in its own chaos, the clergy and people of St. Paul's are an anchor for me.

Dianne Dooley works for the Department of Veterans Affairs as a vocational rehabilitation specialist.

About 8:20 A.M. Karan Shepard called me from the third floor Credit Union and asked me to fill in for a member of the credit committee who was unavailable to keep a scheduled appointment. I serve as a volunteer on that committee, and, although my usual time is Friday mornings, I told Karan I could be there at 9:00.

About 8:55 I told co-worker John Colvin I was leaving and would be back in about thirty minutes. As I started out, John called me back to take a call from Dennis Jackson, another co-worker. It was 9:00 straight up when I finally left. On the way out I said, "I need to hurry. I'm late for the credit union." I headed for the fifth floor's south stairwell and hurriedly skipped down the stairs to the third floor landing. Just as I pushed open the stairwell door there was a BOOM! and the heavy door exploded in on me.

My first thought was, "My God, I've detonated a bomb." The force of it threw me to the ground. I landed between the door opening and the other door leading onto the third floor. I was stunned but conscious. As I stood up I heard a man's voice crying for help. I had no idea where he was, and for some reason I was unable to find my own voice to answer him. For a split second I thought about going back up to the stairs to my office. Then I noticed I had suffered an open fracture to my right wrist. The stairwell was filling with thick, black smoke, causing me to choke, so I decided to get out of the building. I was aware that I had survived whatever it was, and I concentrated on trying to keep calm.

I was familiar with the exits and knew I could walk down one more level and exit to the south. On the way I stepped out of one shoe, which was immediately lost in the smoke and had to be left. I pushed the outside door open and started walking across the courtyard. I was the first person out of the building. Walking had gotten difficult, and my right hand was severely injured with blood spewing from the wrist. I realized I looked a mess, what with the condition of my arm, having only one shoe, and clothes that were torn and bloody. I focused on trying to make it to the street without passing out. When I finally got there, I stood on the corner by the parking garage thinking, "Someone help me!" I must have been in shock, because I still had no voice.

Two gentlemen ran toward me and had me lie down on the pavement. They assured me that help was on the way and, sure enough, within minutes I was loaded into an Oklahoma City police car driven by Officer Erick Thompson. Two more injured were loaded into the car as well, and soon enough we pulled into the emergency entrance at St. Anthony Hospital. We were the first victims to arrive, and as we were wheeled in I noticed the clock in the emergency room showed 9:20 A.M. By 9:45 my family knew both my whereabouts and my status. I had suffered compound fractures to my wrist, index finger, and thumb. I also had a broken right toe.

I never looked back at the building to witness the chaos that took place. I lost a dozen friends and many acquaintances, including Karan Shepard from the credit union. My wrist required four surgeries and more are planned. When I think back, I have to acknowledge that it was the phone call from Dennis Jackson that delayed my trip to the credit union and almost certainly saved my life. The irony is that I am compulsively punctual and, no doubt, would have otherwise arrived downstairs on time.

∞

Karen Patterson is a registered nurse at Presbyterian Hospital.

The devastation I experienced April 19 reminded me of the horrible shrapnel wounds of war I saw as a flight

Above: A FEMA search team works on a fallen beam inside the Murrah Building. — **Photo courtesy of FEMA**

Below: A bucket brigade works diligently to move the mountain of crushed concrete in front of the Federal Building. — **Photo courtesy of FEMA**

nurse, when we air-evacuated wounded soldiers back home from Vietnam. What memories that brought back to mind...

∽

Dudley Hutcheson is a readjustment counseling specialist with the Department of Veterans' Affairs in Oklahoma City.

It has been twenty years since the fall of Saigon and the end of the Vietnam War, and most veterans have managed to put the experience behind them. For some it has been a struggle, but the majority of combat veterans have completed the healing process and now function about as well as anyone. When the Murrah Building was bombed, all the things veterans have been working so hard to overcome literally came crashing down around them. What sense of safety and trust they had re-established was shattered, once again demonstrating that life can be lost in a heartbeat.

Many visitors to the bomb site have said it looked like a war zone. Media coverage has kept the television screen full of explicit pictures of wounded, bleeding, and dazed victims which, to many combat veterans, are gruesome reminders of that horrific war. At least this time, the support will be there.

∽

Vietnam veteran Jim Ross is a co-worker of blast survivor Stan Rombaun.

Stan's body was battered: one eye swollen shut, arms bundled, face battered and scraped. Framed in hospital white, his purple-smeared torso was scratched and gouged and sutured. He looked exactly like somebody wounded in combat. The day before, two agonizing hours had passed between the detonation downtown and the discovery of his

151

whereabouts. For me, they were hours during which the decades-old corpses of Charlie Company conducted a malicious march through my inner graveyard, intent on finding the gate. Trying to shove them back in their graves was useless. I was as helpless to stop them now as I had been to save them in Vietnam. Like Stan and his fellow victims, Charlie's patrol was ambushed in a vulnerable moment, and we couldn't get there in time. An entire platoon had been cut off and overrun before we could fire a single, saving shot. All that remained were the mangled bodies of boys and a shadowy patch of smoldering jungle. Their executioners had vanished.

Within two days of the bombing, I was soaked with sorrow and anger. I had overdosed on the avalanche of reports and images, and, like a return to the televised war, its impact triggered haunting memories that robbed me of sleep and left me bouncing between spells of stoic acceptance and depression. A resurrected sense of hopelessness and the lingering self-accusation that I should have done more, that Vietnam was still unfinished business, taunted and tugged.

I wasn't alone. The local Vet Center got busy. Within my own circle, some talked openly, some stewed silently. My friend Dave called me the first week. He was drunk. His mind burned with the horror of the bombing and the sickening parallel to lives wasted so recklessly in a war that couldn't be won. He had fixated on the idea of going back to Southeast Asia. He couldn't explain why exactly, but he was convinced it was the only chance he'd ever have to slay the dragon. Somehow it made sense, but it wouldn't work for me. I now knew the time-worn longing to heal completely would remain untended, that there would be no permanent peace. Not ever. The corpses of Charlie Company would see to that.

∽

Stan Rombaun, a veterans employment representative for the State of Oklahoma, worked in the Veterans' Administration's fifth floor office. He spent twenty-one days in the hospital.

I was sitting behind my desk with my back to the north window. I have a vague recollection of hearing a *whooomp!* and then a sensation of strong wind. The next thing I knew I was lying on the floor to the right of my desk next to a window that was now gone. A couple more feet and I would've been over the edge.

I had no idea where I was or how I had gotten there. Piles of twisted wreckage were heaped all around me, and the air was filled with dust. My first thought was, *What, am I doing here? I'm supposed to be at work.* I raised my left hand and saw it was covered with blood. My fingers were pointing every which way. I realized my head was also bleeding. I called out, "Somebody help me, will you? Can somebody please help me?" A voice I later recognized as John Colvin called out, "Stan, don't move. Whatever you do, don't move. I'm coming to get you."

I had curled into a fetal position by the time he got to me and started pulling me from the window. He managed to get me up, but I slipped and fell down again. He said, "I'll be right back." A minute later he returned with another co-worker, then some other people came into the area. Somehow they led me to the hallway, where I buckled to the floor again. This was very close to where the floor had broken off. The right side of my face was really bleeding and my vision was impaired, so I wasn't able to comprehend the extent of the destruction. I remember looking up and seeing a couple of firemen. They said, "Don't worry, we'll get you down." And they put me on a stretcher and carried me down three flights of stairs to an exit onto the south patio.

I couldn't feel any pain, just numbness, and I was aware of other hurt people around me once we were outside. I didn't know it yet, but my right eye had been severely damaged and my hand was mangled. Plugs of flesh had been gouged from my legs. On top of it, I had numerous lacerations and was peppered with glass. I could hear sirens, and within minutes I was rushed to St. Anthony Hospital, where I was taken immediately into surgery.

I was in the hospital for three weeks. They operated on my eye again, but I still have only blurred vision. Somehow they pieced all my fingers back together. I got calls and cards and letters from all over the country. The Secretary of Labor called me, and Troy Aikman visited when the Dallas Cowboys were here. I even got an offer from one of my counterparts in Texas to come and cut my grass or do chores until I got out. The support was unbelievable.

When the shock wore off, after a couple of days, I started to feel some emotion, but I didn't know who to get mad at. The whole thing seemed unreal. How the hell could it happen? I didn't read much in the hospital because of my eye, but I knew quite a few people had died. Then a buddy brought up a *Newsweek* with that picture of the fireman and the baby on the cover. Her grandfather, Tommy Almon, cuts my hair. We've known each other for years. He came to see me in the hospital. We both cried. It was Tommy who dropped little Baylee off at the daycare center that morning. What can you say? What in the world can you say?

I still don't know how I feel, but I know something's not right. There's something inside. I don't know what it is, but there's something in there. And I can't get it out.

∞

PART
III

Inch by Inch: The Search for Victims

It was very difficult to distinguish between hope and agony. At times there seemed to be little difference.

Above: Search team members prepare a hole for exploration.
— **Photo courtesy of FEMA**

Below: Workers confer during a break in the ongoing search
and rescue operation. — **Photo courtesy of FEMA**

Oklahoma City firefighter Stephen Davis spent considerable time inside the Murrah Building with Rescue Squad 16.

So many treasures lay scattered through that building: family pictures, Bibles, letters. All of them connected us to the victims. I spotted an American flag that I later learned belonged in the Veterans Administration Office on the fifth floor. It had fallen over, but was not damaged at all. That flag became a symbol for me. It stood for the endurance of all those who came to help and for the ultimate price paid by those who died while in service to America.

∞

William R. Rusk is a lieutenant with the Shawnee, Oklahoma, Fire Department.

Our team formed a bucket brigade and went as far into the Federal Building as we were allowed. We picked up debris and placed it in five-gallon buckets so as not to hurt anyone who might still be trapped in the building. When the buckets were full, we passed them back along the line of men, and they were emptied into a dumpster. All of us had only one goal: to pull someone out of that awful mess alive.

Later that night, at home, I watched televised reports of the rescue efforts. I thought I was handling things well until pictures of the missing children flashed across the screen. I found myself crying then, and an empty feeling filled my heart. I didn't think I could go back, but after talking with my priest, my wife, and my fellow firemen, I felt better. Four days later I was back inside.

The first day back I helped pull out three bodies, two adults and a baby. The second day we removed five more. On my last day there I helped recover another four.

I know none of us who were in that building will ever be the same. We keep thinking, "If we could have just brought one person out alive. Just one." Even though we know we did everything we could, sometimes it seems like there is something not quite finished, something left undone.

∞

Suzi Sharp is an administrative assistant at the Oklahoma City-based charity Feed the Children.

I discovered the man who had been working beside me was from Minnesota. He was here on vacation to help. The van we unloaded came from Wisconsin, driven by two young women. Behind it was a truck from upstate New York, followed by others from Kentucky and California and Arkansas and North Carolina and Maine. Other trucks, filled with safety boots and respirators and various supplies, had rolled in from Colorado. It started in a small community north of Denver. Soon it was a caravan of four semi-tractor trailers.

∞

Pete Gutzmann is a firefighter and EMT with White Bear Fire and Rescue in White Bear Lake, Minnesota.

I talked with my wife, Micky, about noon on April 19, and she was quite distraught. She told me what had happened in Oklahoma City. I thought about it during the day and watched it on TV that night. Thursday morning I was still thinking about it and wishing there was something I could do. Thursday evening, while watching the news about 10:15 P.M., my wife came in and looked at me and said, "Are you going to go, or what?" I called my fellow firefighter, Jeff Zentzis, and we decided to go help. We were on our way to Oklahoma by midnight. We drove through a blizzard in southern Minnesota. It took thirteen hours to make the trip.

∞

Lieutenant Jeff Zentzis is a firefighter and EMT with White Bear Lake Fire and Rescue in White Bear Lake, Minnesota.

Fellow firefighter Pete Gutzmann called me on Thursday evening and suggested we leave right away to go help in Oklahoma City. We were on the road within one and a half hours. We drove through a fierce blizzard in southern Minnesota to get there. Round trip was over 1,600 miles.

The hospitality in Oklahoma City was incredible! There was one area set up strictly for supplies. They had gloves, knees pads, underwear, you name it. They told us to get whatever we needed. We were planning to sleep on cots in a nearby garage; however, the Midwest City Fire Department insisted we stay at their station house. Everyone treated us in an outstanding manner. I only wish I could have done more inside the building.

∞

Annie Lerum is a search dog handler who deployed with her furry partner, Colter, as part of the Sacramento FEMA Task Force on April 19.

We did an eighteen-hour blitz starting Thursday morning. We searched the basement and the first and second floors. Then we were loaned to the Oklahoma City Fire Department to search the third and fourth floors.

The bottom two floors were so compacted it was mostly unrecognizable. The upper floors, however, still had sweaters hanging on the backs of chairs and photos of families on the desktops. It really personalized the loss. I found a yellow Post-it note that said something like, "Pick up Christie after school." I prayed that she had gotten out and been able to do that.

We stayed in the Southwestern Bell offices. The president, David Lopez, opened his private office to us and the single shower was made available to all the rescuers. He would go around in the evening vacuuming the carpets.

∞

Officer Michael Adams is a patrolman with the Mustang, Oklahoma, Police Department.

I was off duty when the call came. We were told to report to the command post at 9th and Broadway. Our job was mainly traffic control, making sure everyone we let in had a reason to be there. My part, keeping onlookers and gawkers out, was surely microscopic compared to what the other guys were doing. I was just glad to do what I could. As confusing as it all was, there was no looting or anything.

I remember a baby that was lying on the sidewalk the first day. They had laid it on the curb on the north side of the building. It wasn't until I had time to sit back and think about it that it really hit me.

∞

Lieutenant John Clark is with the Oklahoma City Police Department.

All of the Emergency Response Team members were given one day off out of the seventeen days we were involved. The men and women of that unit will never be the same. No one who was involved will be. Because I had so much time and effort invested in the unit, I took a special interest in it. I saw these officers torn with anger and tears, yet they never once complained. They were so proud to do their job. It will surely prove to be one of the toughest assignments they will encounter in their careers. I am so very, very proud of them.

∞

Justin Adams is a member of the Oklahoma Army National Guard.

Our unit worked security. Sometimes people would just lift up the crime scene tape and go underneath it like it wasn't even there. Photographers, like that. One guy was dressed up in uniform—ID badge, wearing the rank of captain. He was a reporter. He was arrested and taken to jail. At one time I heard there were eight reporters in jail. None of them local.

We also worked at the Medical Examiner's Office. Our job was to keep the bodies in order. We'd take them off the truck for x-rays, then put them back on. We did that for about three hours one day. I'm a volunteer fireman, but I've never had to do anything of that magnitude.

∽

Dr. Sheila Simpson is an Oklahoma City physician.

I had to do something. Because my husband is a policeman, a big part of my practice involves people in those professions. I wanted to do something to help them as they patrolled the area and risked their lives during the rescue and recovery process.

I called some drug representatives, who come to my office. They got their companies to donate sample drugs. I was taken into the area, where I was able to set up a "cardboard clinic" at the Southwestern Bell Building. We had everything imaginable, from antibiotics and surgical supplies to decongestants and laxatives, all of it donated. If there was anything that any of the workers needed, all it took was a phone call. One store didn't have the kind of shoe pads we needed, but they sent other supplies they thought we could use and helped locate the pads we were looking for. It was like that with everyone we called: doctor's offices, supply houses, stores. You name it. Everybody in the state of Okla-

161

homa, the whole country for that matter, wanted to help any way they could.

At the clinic I treated lacerations, blood blisters, and bleeding feet, but the best treatment I gave was to hug somebody whose heart was hurting, some police officer or firefighter or volunteer who had seen too much and needed a human touch to keep going. I gave out as many hugs as I did pills.

Every day when I got home I sat and sobbed, not just for the pain and suffering I'd seen, but for the incredible outpouring of generosity and love I'd witnessed. Knowing the person or not didn't matter. Everyone reached out to each other. I'm so humbled and grateful to have been a part of it. So much goodness has come from such a horrible, evil deed. We will all be stronger because of this.

∞

Rodney LeRoy is in the Air Force, stationed at Tinker Air Force Base near Oklahoma City.

The feeling of total chaos and confusion, mixed with the sound of silent death, ran through me while we worked. Every person there seemed to be drained of emotion—like zombies. To me, they resembled troops of a lost war with no one to turn to.

∞

Jack West is a salesman for Olympus Corporation, which provided fiber optic medical equipment to aid in the building search.

As soon as I heard what happened, I contacted the Federal Emergency Management Agency (FEMA) and offered the use of our scopes. By Thursday we had rushed all the equipment FEMA had asked for. I was honored to help as a consultant at the scene. It was a privilege working with the search and rescue teams, although it was heartbreaking at the same time.

I came out from under that building and saw Oklahomans rush to console, feed and thank those rescue workers. I've been in many circles of people, even played professional football, but these people topped them all.

∽

Major David A. Dalberg is with the Salvation Army in Minneapolis, Minnesota.

Arrangements were made for me to visit Salvation Army services at the site of the "pit." After going through several check points, my escort and I arrived at the gate. Security had tightened, but after a brief discussion with FBI personnel we were admitted. Even as we approached ground zero I could feel my stomach begin to tighten. I watched rescue personnel painstakingly lift and remove rubble, bucket after bucket after bucket. The "pit" was a disaster site. The "pit" was a rescue site. The "pit" was also a crime scene. Every bucketful was sifted and every piece of material was examined for evidence. The process was an arduous effort for rescuers and federal agents, as well.

It was very difficult to distinguish between hope and agony. At times there seemed to be little difference. I watched two rugged-looking Salvation Army volunteers. They were Vietnam veterans and had probably seen their share of tragedy. They responded to whatever requests were made of them. Their ministry was not filled with words, but it was as though their lives were the very hands of God reaching out to touch and serve those who struggled in their rescue and recovery efforts.

After returning to one of the canteens, I thought I heard someone crying. The sound was soft and quiet. I questioned whether I was really hearing it. As I moved along the driver's side of the canteen, I found another worker, John, with his face buried in his hands. I moved close to him and put my hand on his shoulder. He turned to me, tears streaming down his face. There were no words; nothing would suffice for the moment. All I could do was put my arms around him and hold him. His cries became louder. Within seconds he started to wail, his voice filling the air with pain. For the first time during my nine-day duty, I was torn by the depth of emotions that so many, in so many different ways, had to face.

∽

Phil Burrow is an Alva, Oklahoma, firefighter.

First, I was teamed with a group of firefighters from Warr Acres. We retrieved computers from the fifth floor and helped remove debris from the front of the building. Later I worked with two Oklahoma City firefighters. As we dug, we began finding business cards belonging to a woman who had worked in the Secret Service office. As we dug further, we found her checkbook, then her body. She was pinned by a large slab of concrete. We had to mark the spot and leave her there.

∽

Oscar Johnson is the general manager of Mid-Western Elevator.

Several of our service representatives assisted the firemen and the General Services Administration inspector to check all seven elevators in the Murrah Building. While inside, they came across dead and dying people and helped transport some of the children in an attempt to same them. A few of the transported children were dead. The service men were very distraught, given the conditions, and their ability to concentrate was a concern. We took extra precau-

Top photo:
Red Cross volunteers
Michelle Friedel and
Hal McKnight.
— **Photo courtesy of**
Hal McKnight

Right photo:
Cards and letters sent
by caring children
cover
a supply room wall.
— **Photo courtesy of**
Hal McKnight

tions by reminding the men that it was a very tenuous time and to be extra vigilant of hazardous conditions. We also paired them up with each other.

By 6:00 P.M. on April 20, we had a running elevator platform. At this point we reinforced the walls at the first and second floors for running clearance on the elevator. We took the #5 hoistway doors in the basement and used them on the second landing of elevator #1. All other doors of the #1 elevator were repaired in place. All safety devices were tested on the elevator. Elevator #1 was placed in service at approximately 7:00 A.M. on April 21. Firemen were then able to begin using it for transportation of personnel.

At 10:00 A.M. the same morning the fire chief asked what it would take to get the freight elevator operational. We inspected it, and it was determined that if the debris from two fallen walls could be moved and wooden barricades built at each landing, the freight elevator could be placed in service as well. The fire chief assigned two work crews to the elevator people and had the areas cleaned up by 6:00 P.M. We rebuilt the elevator and had it operational by 3:00 P.M. the next day. Both elevators remained in service throughout the recovery.

∽

Steve Fayfitch is a service representative with Mid-Western Elevator. He arrived at the building at 1:00 P.M. on April 19.

We began a survey of the damage, hoping we could put at least one of the elevators into operation. We found doors missing and doors hanging from their tracks, but the elevators seemed to be in usable condition.

We selected the northeast elevator as the one to get going. We worked as hard and as fast as safety would allow. At times we stood on wooden beams as high as four floors in the air while our crews removed doors and door tracks. We tied safety belts onto anything solid.

Oklahoma Gas and Electric supplied wire over the top of the building, and Bloom Electric supplied a diesel generator for power. Our crews modified wiring on the elevator control panel to isolate the one we were repairing, taking special precautions to make sure that safety devices were working.

On the third day of the operation I got my first real look at the building's heavily damaged north side. I saw the personal effects of people that I knew probably didn't survive. I saw rescue workers digging with their hands, and I saw the look of disappointment on their faces when they found a body instead of a survivor.

What I will remember always is the way Oklahoma and the world responded. There were more supplies than we could use, more food and drink than we could ever consume, and more love than I have ever seen.

∞

Joni Hale is from Moore, Oklahoma. She was in downtown Oklahoma City on the morning of April 19.

Pam Mize from my office organized us to go to the Myriad and work for the Red Cross. It was great. I finally got to help! All of us really enjoyed getting to go. Later, during a break, we walked down toward the site. At first I felt like turning around and running back, but I continued on. Then we reached the little area that had the flowers, pictures, poems and teddy bears in it, and I couldn't hold it any longer. Tears ran down my face, and my legs got weak. I felt like I was about to pass out. What held me up was my determination to finish helping at the Red Cross.

∞

Dr. Steve Watson has been practicing medicine in Oklahoma City for fifteen years.

On Thursday another doctor and I decided to try and get permission to go down to the building. It had become obvious that any survivors found by then would need on-the-spot care. Early Friday morning found us at the site and ready to go to work.

My initiation came early. We had just arrived when I was directed to treat the Medical Examiner. He had collapsed on the scene from dehydration and exhaustion. He was the first of many with the same condition.

Optimistically, I told one of the firemen from Phoenix, "You find 'em, we'll save 'em." We were all dejected when, one by one, the "found" were beyond saving.

The rescuers kept on working until ordered out of the building, even at risk to their own health and well-being. We treated sprained ankles and twisted knees. We irrigated and treated eyes that were damaged by every imaginable foreign object. We treated colds, sinus infections, and bronchitis. Some representatives from pharmaceutical companies made sure that we had what we needed to treat injured and ill rescuers. Incredibly, no matter how uncomfortable or ill the rescuers became, they didn't leave. They were driven by an incredible sense of purpose that masked exhaustion, hunger, and sickness.

We realized early on that everyone working in the building would need a tetanus shot. We coordinated with the Red Cross to get that taken care of. Every worker who came out of the building lined up to get a tetanus shot, until they had all been vaccinated.

Friday night we were called into the building with the horrifying words: "Two firemen are down!" The probable reasons for those words were more terrible than I could think about. I was relieved when I discovered their collapse was due to the now familiar "dehydration and exhaustion."

The second time I went into the building was Sunday night. By then things had gotten pungent. The odor of death is unlike anything else. Even if you have never smelled it, there is no doubt what it is. It's a quick, penetrating, stomach-turning odor. It was making the rescue workers physically ill. We were able to get some ointment from some of the funeral homes to put under their noses and help mask the odor.

By Monday morning the mood of everyone began to change. Hope for finding survivors had dwindled. The realization came to each one of us sometime that night that there were no more survivors. The focus then went from rescuing survivors to recovering victims. This realization was intensely depressing and enveloped the area with gloom.

Through it all, though, there was a bonding among us. I became friends with rescuers from Kansas City, Topeka, and Phoenix, as well as with an ATF agent from Washington, D.C. Governor Keating stopped by twice. He was not only an impressive representative of Oklahomans to the nation, but also a source of comfort to all of us there—a lifeline to sanity.

Jim Parker is a deputy United States marshal assigned to Salt Lake City. He served as a member of the stress debriefing team in Oklahoma City.

Marshal Service personnel lost two family members to the bomb. A child and a wife of two of our employees died in this tragedy. It was like we had all lost two of our own family members.

I was not there when the child was located, but I was there when Kathy was finally located. On Thursday, April 27, there was news that the rescue teams might have located her. As sad as we all were, we knew it was going to help her family to find her and get her out of the building. At 4:30 P.M. I peered into the pit from up above, as a team of men and women attempted to retrieve the body of a female. We knew what Kathy was wearing on her last day at work. We also had a good description of her wedding ring and what she looked like.

All we could see at first were a woman's legs and her right arm. We were in the ball game when it came to the clothes, but we could not get a look at her face nor were we able to see her left hand. We were hoping this was her, but we were not sure. The crews in the pit knew we were hoping. They would come out every so often and tell us that they were giving it their best, and that "it should be soon."

At first we were thankful that this might be coming to an end, but hour after hour we kept hearing "soon." Nevertheless, these brave men and women kept a frantic, yet controlled pace. They would dig and dig, stop and cut more metal, then dig and dig again. Never stopping, never complaining.

More hours passed. Then around 10:00 P.M. we were at last in a position to see the ring or face of the woman we prayed was our Kathy. Our supervisors, friends of Kathy's husband, gathered all marshal personnel for a briefing. We were told that if this was Kathy, we would place her body in one of those black body bags, a United States flag would be placed over her. She would then be marched out of the pit and to the make-shift medical examiner's tent by only the Marshal Service. We were all quiet during this briefing. You could feel the tension as every one of us hoped that this part of our mission was soon to be over.

A team of eight Marshal personnel went back in for the actual extraction. I lost sight of our team as they disappeared around the corner into the pit. A short time passed and then, ever so slowly, they came back with the body of the lady we had all grown so close to. A flag was draped over her body and the gurney was wheeled to a stop.

As we lined up and started off, the rescue team that had worked so hard at uncovering her stood alongside with their masks off and their helmets over their hearts. They just stared at us. Someone stopped the procession long enough so this brave rescue team could join in to march the body out of the building and to the Medical Examiner's tent.

The underground parking garage was dark and musty, and there was dampness to it. As we exited into daylight, there stood, to our surprise, a large number of military, police, and ATF agents. They were all at attention, staring straight ahead, and saluting the flag and the lady under it.

They didn't know who she was. They didn't have to. All they knew was that the body beneath that flag meant something to the United States Marshal Service. And she did.

Eight Marshal personnel entered the Medical Examiner's tent and closed the makeshift door behind them. We all then waited for the verdict. When they came out, the looks on their faces told us that we had our Kathy. No one had to say a word. We had waited over two days for this news. Though thankful, there were no celebrations, or even smiles, just a lot of tears and crying.

∽

Jeff Welsh is president of Magnum Foods, Oklahoma franchisee for Little Caesar's Pizza. The firm established a twenty-four-hour pizzeria at the site and fed workers free for two weeks.

We cooked hot pizza under a tent roof twenty-four hours a day from the Thursday following the blast until Tuesday, May 2. To break the monotony of pizza, we cooked donated cinnamon rolls in the pizza ovens for breakfast. We gave an estimated 8,500 pizzas during that time, and half again as many cinnamon rolls.

We were never at loss for volunteers from our company, and some brought their spouses or friends. When the weather turned coarse, they huddled in front of the ovens with blankets on their laps, waiting for a firefighter or Red Cross worker or anyone else to come along. Then they jumped up and hustled to get them a hot slice or a whole box of pizza. We were proud to serve these amazing workers who spent their time on their hands and knees across the street.

At night the building glowed under the intense spotlights, and you could plainly see the rescuers climbing the three-story-high pile of cement and twisted metal. When they finished their shift, many walked out of the gate guarding the building and headed our way to quietly ask for a piece of pizza. Many of them refused seconds and thanked us over and over for our concern and generosity and for just being there. To these "thank yous" we never ceased to be amazed. The contrast was powerful: our sidewalk pizzeria versus their somber task.

∽

Major Rita Aragon is the commander of the 137th Logistics Squadron of the Oklahoma Air National Guard. She is also the principal of Western Village Elementary in Oklahoma City.

Thursday morning, April 20, I reported to the First Christian Church at 7:00 A.M. to serve on the notification team with nineteen Army and Air National Guard Chaplains. Twelve- and fourteen-hour days soon seemed to run together. At one point I was walking past the church's office, when the secretary reached out and touched my arm. She said, "I have a phone call for a military person." The lady on the phone identified herself, through sobs, as the aunt of a four-year-old little girl. The parents of the child had been in the Army Recruiter's office the morning of the blast. The mother was in serious condition, the father in intensive care. A younger child had been found unharmed, but the mother was inconsolable because there had been no word on her four-year-old daughter. I told the aunt that the Medical Examiner could not release any information, but I would see if I could find out something for her. The aunt stressed that she had already checked the hospitals, but had no success. She was so afraid the little girl was unconscious in a hospital or, worse yet, too terrified by the ordeal to tell anyone her name. I took her number and name and promised to do what I could.

I found the information to help the family, but what help was this? The ultimate closure. The gentleman sitting across from me looked very gently into my eyes and said, "Are you OK?" I said, "Yes, but how much can I tell this

172

poor woman?" He said, "Well, you can't tell her that the child is dead."

I called the number at the hospital that the aunt had given me. I identified myself and told her again that I was not allowed to confirm death, only the Medical Examiner could do that. "However," I added very slowly and softly, "I can tell you that you may stop looking for your niece in the hospitals. She isn't there."

I got a most unexpected reaction. She sobbed, "Oh, thank you. We just had to know she wasn't lying somewhere hurt, lonely, and afraid." Again and again, she thanked me, her words burning my ears and my heart. "Thank you" for telling her a precious life was gone? But this was why I was there, why I kept making all those calls and contacts. The closure was critical. Only then could the grieving begin.

∞

Lynn Ricks is with Sonic Drive-Ins.

On April 21, while handing out coffee at 5th Street and Harvey, I met firemen from all of the states that had sent help. One firefighter from Phoenix told a remarkable story of how their fire and rescue unit arranged to obtain money to come here. After raising as much as they could, the firemen contacted Southwest Airlines and asked if the amount they had would get all of them to Oklahoma City to help search for survivors. Southwest responded with a "no" to that amount of money. However, if the firemen were going to Oklahoma City to help, Southwest would fly them for free. Upon arrival, the firemen found limousines waiting and were taken by police escort to their hotel, which would not take their money, either.

When I delivered food to the County Sheriff's post at 10th and Robinson, I handed lunch to a lady sheriff from Dade County, Florida. She asked me how much she owed me for it, and I told her "nothing." A pastor from out of town kept walking around with a $1 bill sticking out of his shirt pocket. He said no one would let him spend it, no matter how many times he offered to pay.

ᑫᑫᑎ

R.N. Pam Love works in the emergency room at Oklahoma City's Southwest Medical Center.

I had the opportunity to help volunteers downtown in a medical booth where different drugs, suntan lotions, lip ointment, toiletries, and so on were offered. We had so many supplies, and they were all donated by the hospitals, local businesses, and individuals. I saw a lot of workers who were mentally, physically, and emotionally drained.

There were many different ways that people helped. One lady from Kansas made fresh cookies early one morning and brought them down. Two of my neighbors, three restaurants, and our own cafeteria brought food to the hospital emergency room during the disaster. Citizens called or came by to see if they could help in any way, even to offer free baby-sitting service.

ᑫᑫᑎ

Kegy Ruark arrived with his portable barbecue wagon in downtown Oklahoma City from his home base in Vinita, Oklahoma, within hours of the explosion. For more than forty-eight hours he gave away food and drink.

At 10:00 A.M. on April 19, I walked into my business, Charlie's BBQ, as I do everyday. Little did I know the next words I'd hear would change me and thousands of others forever.

"You hear about the bomb?" an employee asked me.

"What bomb?" I said.

Above: A broken slab of cement became the cornerstone for this poignant bomb site memorial.

— Photo courtesy of Steve Fayfitch

Below: Work crews sift through loose debris inside the Murrah Building. **— Photo courtesy of Penny Turpen James**

"A bomb went off, killed six kids in a day care center. It's on the radio. Listen," he said.

I was horrified at what I heard. Hundreds killed, hundreds more injured. They were pleading for all available medical personnel to report. I knew it was something like we had never seen, and I thought my services could be used.

I'm a cook, not a doctor. However, I do know CPR and first aid. I am in the habit of feeding large numbers of people outdoors against the Oklahoma elements, which can change without warning. It is very different than feeding people in a sheltered, controlled environment. I have a self-contained mobile unit.

I immediately asked Ed to start filling the ice chests. We loaded enough barbecue, hamburger, pop and coffee for about 1,000 people. I had no idea what was in store for me or whether I would make it in the old '75. I also didn't know if they would let me in once I got there.

Linda Hatcher, of the local Red Cross, tried for two hours to get authorization for me, but could only tell me that she couldn't tell me whether to stay or go. With that, I said I was going, and she wished me luck.

After a tense ride to Oklahoma City—200 miles—I arrived, not knowing what would happen next. Exits were blocked, so I got off the interstate at the first one open and entered the city. It was a windy, stormy night—with a lot of lightning. This, added to the sirens and emergency lights, made for quite a stimulating effect as I drove toward the downtown area. When I got closer to the site, the police made me drive further away. Finally, I stopped in the middle of an intersection and a policeman yelled for me "to get that rig outta the way."

I explained I had food and drinks. He said, "Make me a sandwich and I'll let you in. I've been here since nine o'clock this morning and haven't had anything to eat or drink." He yelled to another policeman to move a barricade and let me in. I then pulled over to the side, and two officers entered my trailer with flashlights. They were so hungry they wanted to eat the barbecue cold.

I found them some warm barbecue and made them

sandwiches and coffee. They were much obliged. Then I drove off to find the Red Cross. It was a very congested area, so when I found an empty place I pulled in. It was behind a business called Radio Supply, Inc. A man approached and asked me if I needed any help. He said his name was Craig, and he wanted to help. I said, "Sure."

We were both in awe of the spectacle displayed in front of us at the Alfred Murrah Building only one and a half blocks away. Being curious, we walked toward the building and cut down an alley. The next thing we knew we were in a nightmare war zone. With every footstep glass crunched under our feet. Building and car parts littered the streets and sidewalks.

We came to the crime scene tape stretched around the perimeter, so we turned around, only to find they wouldn't let us out of the area. The police explained that no one was going in or out. When I told him about the trailer, he let us through. En route we had to cross another barrier, and when we got back to the trailer, I decided to stay put.

I sent Craig to check in with the Red Cross, and we were warmly welcomed. They informed us they would be by in about twenty minutes and asked us to please make all the sandwiches we could for them to deliver to the rescue workers. They came, took several dozen barbecue sandwiches, and said they would return for more around 2:00 or 3:00 A.M.

Craig stayed and helped me until 1:00 or 2:00 A.M., then left. I served food and coffee all night long to Southwestern Bell linemen, volunteers, and technicians from the media. It was really something to see everything unfold. Still, it was a long, sad night.

Daylight came Thursday morning with an eerie quietness. I was in a restricted area, but far enough from the cranes and generators to hear the birds chirping and singing. That didn't last long, though, as the place soon filled up with people. NBC had set up next to me during the night. Cameras were everywhere. Also, Governor Keating and Senator Nickles were there very early, surveying the situation. Congressman J. C. Watt's secretary vowed to get me anything I needed, though I assured her I was doing fine.

Several hours later, when I was getting low on supplies and thinking of calling her, a medical student named Shawn showed up wanting to help me. He went to the grocery store after I gave him—a perfect stranger—a handful of money. He returned three hours later, having spent about $100 of his own. While he was gone, a couple from Blanchard showed up with two ice chests full of hamburgers from their own freezer. I was very grateful. They said they had seen me on TV, and I looked like I needed help.

Some people from El Reno brought me hot dogs and buns. One woman, who had lost two family members in the blast, baked a big sheet of brownies and brought them to me. Another woman named Jo Kubic from Marlow showed up to help cook. A young man named Ricky came and helped cook all day, all night, and into Friday. Leonard White, an Oklahoma City businessman, also showed up to help. It was he who made arrangements to bring another concession rig in to replace mine when I had to leave on Friday.

I felt I had accomplished what I had set out to do and then some. But all the while I kept thinking of those who were trapped, and I wished I could be there to help dig or somehow be actively involved. As a result of my contribution I received many "thank you" cards and money from people I know and don't know from all over. I was overwhelmed by all the people thanking me for what I did. A Sunday school class sent me a batch of pictures that each child had taken time to draw. That was really touching.

cro

Lee Brouwer, an engineer with the Federal Aviation Administration, donated his time and his knowledge of cooking to the on-going food service effort.

I worked as a volunteer for the Oklahoma Restaurant Association during the disaster. The ORA had set up a food

178

preparation area and serving line for the rescuers at the Myriad Convention Center. UPS provided trucks and volunteer drivers to deliver food, workers, and supplies to the bomb site perimeter. When I first approached ORA officials I told them I had cooked all my life but never as a profession. "Can you work nights?" was all they asked.

On April 24 I was asked if I would relocate to the Disaster Command Post food service area in the parking garage at 8th and Harvey and keep it going. What had started out as a 150-meal operation was now approaching 500, with the promise of going much higher. They explained that the ORA chefs working there had to get back to their regular jobs.

I was not sure I could do it and hesitated. The last thing I wanted was to fail the rescuers. Then they told me I was the only full-time volunteer available. They also promised to provide me with plenty of good volunteers, so I agreed. And did they ever keep their word! The two hundred plus food service people who worked shifts at 8th and Harvey were dedicated beyond belief. For the next nine days, we provided twenty-four-hour hot food service. Not one person came to our line without getting a hot meal. Plate counts averaged 1,100 for breakfast, 1,450 for lunch, and 1,000 for dinner. We did this in an open air parking garage, all volunteers, everything donated.

When it was over, I was awarded memberships in both the American Culinary Society and Culinary Arts of Oklahoma.

∽

Milton Bates is a massage therapist for Therapeutic Services Group. He volunteered his time and skill to ease the rescue workers' aches and pains.

A young man approached my massage chair with drooped shoulders and sad countenance. Concrete dust covered his boots, hard hat, and protective clothing. Few words were exchanged, but I could read the body language that spoke of extreme physical and emotional exhaustion.

He had been searching for hours, hoping to find someone who had survived under the massive pile of twisted steel bars and broken concrete. He began to shed his outer clothing, placing the items in a sizable pile beside the massage chair. He then slumped with resignation and relief against the chest pad and face cradle.

I placed my hands on his muscular shoulders. Every thread of his T-shirt was soaked with perspiration, even though the temperature had dropped to the mid-thirties on that unseasonably cold April morning.

Almost immediately, I was able to locate the areas of muscle spasm and pain. As I worked on his neck, back, shoulders, and arms, he fell into a deep sleep. After twenty minutes, I quietly slipped away, leaving him to snooze. When other massage therapists arrived to work the 6:00 A.M. to noon shift, he was still sleeping.

∾

Michael Jay Fagel is a member of the National Alliance for Fire and Emergency Management and works with the Fire Rescue Department in North Aurora, Illinois. He spent four days in Oklahoma as part of an on-site safety team.

After a briefing, I began maneuvering through the site and providing input. Darkness within, shifting debris, the weather, rain, and wind all added to the dilemma, and we soon faced the stark reality that chances of making real rescues diminished more and more as each minute ticked by. I felt like I was walking in a cemetery or walking on tombstones. In the wreckage I saw purses, wallets with photos, personal calendars, name plates from doors and desks, kids' drawings, toys, shoes, even a teddy bear. It was pure sensory overload, and the smell of death was in the air.

∽

Dolores Marie Stratton worked in the United States Army Recruiting office on the fourth floor. Her husband, Charles Stratton, penned these thoughts on May 21.

Friends from work took me to the First Christian Church so we could get more information. I don't know how long we were there. Each time the folks there read lists of the injured, all the people who were missing loved ones held their breaths. With growing horror, I realized that Dee was still missing after fourteen hours had gone by. When told that the center would not receive any more information that night, we returned home. I finally succumbed to exhaustion and fell asleep around 2:00 A.M., only to awaken at 4:00 A.M. My friend was asleep on the couch, so I took the phone and went into the bathroom to call the hospitals again. Each one gave the same answer: no one by that name had been treated or admitted. That was when I knew Dee would never come home again.

A blinding numbness took over. I knew that the only thing left to do was to notify the family and await the official notification by the Army. However, I could not make myself do it, so my dear friend took over for me. I was overcome with despair and grief. On Friday of the same week, the Army came to the house, and I wailed and sobbed like a lost child. I told them to go away. If they did, it wouldn't be true, she wouldn't be dead. Her commanding officer began, "On behalf of the . . ." That was the last thing I heard.

My life has been, for the most part, destroyed. Dee and I were married for eleven and a half years, and we were everything to each other. My life will go on, but without joy, love, and fire.

∽

John Welsch is a paramedic with the Phoenix Fire Department's Urban Search and Rescue Team and a member of FEMA Task Force 1.

It was 11:00 P.M. The rain had stopped, and our first assignment was the second-floor nursery. I left the logistics center and walked toward the most hellish disaster I'd ever faced. With every gust of wind, paper and debris filled the air from the upper stories. Car-sized chunks of concrete, suspended from steel threads, swung precariously over the anthill of workers.

I found my gaze drawn to what was a large and well-equipped playground at the southeast corner of the building. I entered the second floor. It looked like someone had put the contents of a kindergarten into a blender, added some construction material, and turned it on high before unloading it on the floor of this building.

∽

Susan Haas Poston worked as a volunteer for the American Red Cross.

I learned that there is no such thing as just a volunteer. I was touched by the compassion of complete strangers reaching out to help, like the little girl who offered a handful of bandages through a car window to Cindy Wall-Morrison of KOCO-TV, because "bandages fix everything."

One of the few days it wasn't raining I went down to the site to reflect for a few minutes. A woman, obviously distraught, saw my Red Cross ID tags. She asked if I could escort her. This lovely woman, Caroline Murphy, was the aunt of Carrie Ann Lenz, the twenty-six-year-old pregnant victim who worked for the DEA on the ninth floor. She had driven in from Kingman, Arizona, and wanted to see where her niece had spent the last few moments of her life.

Mrs. Murphy told me Carrie had received a sonogram the day before the bombing. She was to have a baby boy.

This aunt then pulled an envelope from her purse. "Would you like to see our Christmas pictures?" she asked.

Between prints, Mrs. Murphy proceeded to tell me about the great reunion they'd had on that holiday. "Carrie was so full of life," her aunt explained. "She was excited about her job, her marriage, her pregnancy."

The happy memories soon faded from Mrs. Murphy's eyes, as we gained a view of what was left of the Federal Building's ninth floor.

∞

Diane Leonard was the wife of Secret Service Agent Donald Leonard, a victim.

The uncertainty of the waiting was the most emotionally draining part of the ordeal. I realized that it would take a miracle for my husband to be found alive, but I kept hoping for that miracle. Then on Friday, April 21, I was asked for Don's dentist's name—they needed his dental records. I began to feel a fear and weight inside my body that I had never felt before. Around 6:30 P.M. that evening I saw four men in suits walking up to my front door, and I knew the uncertainty had come to an end. That is when hope ended and a pain beyond description began.

I am just beginning to fully realize how fragmented my life became on April 19, 1995. All I can do is take it one day at a time and struggle to make some sense of the pieces that remain.

∞

Mike Brake is a former police reporter. He is chief writer for Oklahoma Governor Frank Keating.

I saw the first television images in my office at the Capitol. At first I thought: natural gas explosion. But when the helicopter pulled back and showed the front of the building my immediate fear was: car bomb—maybe a whole van full.

The Governor's press office was unbelievable for the next three days. We didn't have time to log calls, but we must have received a thousand or more a day. At one point I was running between phones talking to a radio station in Christchurch, New Zealand, and a newspaper in Budapest, Hungary. I was getting giddy. I remember telling the Hungarian reporter, "Sure glad you all got rid of communism over there." He probably thought I was an idiot, but he was polite about it: "Tank you, tank you."

The networks were calling: We need the Governor on CNN, Today, Good Morning America, NBC news, CBS, everyone. Larry King was on the phone. Thank goodness our people in the field had pagers.

On Saturday, three days after the bombing, I was driving up Classen in a total daze. I hadn't been out in the daylight and didn't realize everyone was driving with their headlights on in honor of the missing and the dead. Down here we pull over when a funeral approaches. I started to pull to the curb. I thought, this is the biggest funeral procession I've ever seen. It was.

We started planning the Sunday prayer service sometime late Thursday. I knew the Governor and the First Lady would be speaking, and I usually prepare their remarks. What do you say to the whole world about this immense, God-awful event? I went home around midnight Thursday and tried to sleep. At 2:00 I got up with a pen and pad and sat on the sofa and said: Just write it for the people in Oklahoma. So I did. I was pacing the back of the arena when they got up to speak. The first letters were overwhelming. I realized that I'd written something good, something that might outlast the moment. I wrote it from their hearts.

There was a moment, just before the national TV cut into the prayer service, when something wonderful happened. One of the search dog teams, a young woman and her German shepherd, both in orange vests, trotted down the center aisle and the crowd went wild. The President was welcomed very warmly, but (I thought later) a woman and a

184

Above: A pathway is cleared on one of the Federal Building's remaining floors. **— Photo courtesy of Penny Turpen James**

Below: An ATF agent contemplates the rubble-filled crater left by the bomb's detonation.
— Photo courtesy of Steve Fayfitch

dog got the biggest hand of the day. There was something so right about that.

∽

Remarks of First Lady Cathy Keating at the Oklahoma City Prayer Service, Sunday, April 23, 1995.

A little more than 100 hours ago our state was a quiet and happy place. No one could have dreamed that today we would be gathered in such numbers—or in such limitless grief.

We have come here today for prayer, and to begin a time of healing. Our community, our state, and our country have responded to this tragedy with strength and nobility and courage. Today we come together again, with hope and gratitude—and with many, many tears.

We are honored to be joined by distinguished guests, come to share our pain and our hopes. We are grateful to those who have given their talents and artistry to this service. We thank the clergy of our state, who have been pillars of strength and solace to so many in this terrible time.

And we embrace those most directly touched by tragedy.

There are many recovering victims of the blast with us this afternoon. Their outer wounds are still visible—and so are those inside. Others lie in hospitals or at home, too seriously hurt to attend. Our prayers are with them.

To the family members of the dead, the hurt and the missing, we offer our tears and our deepest sympathy. Many of them have joined us, as well. They know that three million Oklahomans are hugging them at this moment. Their grief and their uncertainty is terrible. But they can be certain of one thing: our love.

The rescuers and the helpers are here, too. Never have we seen such a noble blending of courage and compassion. From the first seconds after the blast to this very minute, in all weather, day and night, they have worked to save and to

186

comfort and to protect. Some have come from far away. We honor them all today as true heroes and heroines. From now on, whenever you see a policeman or firefighter or a disaster worker, thank them.

Finally, our children: some are dead, some are missing, and all of them, no matter where they may have been on Wednesday morning, are wounded. It is a terrible crime to steal a child's trust in the goodness of humanity. We have to hold our children close through the nightmares to come. We have to teach them that evil is not the norm. We begin that process today.

But our healing will not come in a day, or a week, or even a year. Our wounds are deep and our scars will be raw. We will each find our separate paths to healing, but we can and must begin that journey together.

I am so grateful to those who are with us today, both in the arena and by radio and television. On this day of mourning Oklahoma comes together. Together we will make a brighter tomorrow—for our victims, for our children, and for all of us who have been deeply touched by tragedy.

∞

Judy Barnett is an American Red Cross volunteer.

I was assigned to work in a canteen area. We served candy, cookies, donuts, pop, and anything else snackwise you could think of. I talked to some of the out-of-state rescuers. They were in awe of all the State of Oklahoma had done for them in the way of made-up beds with mints on the pillows, *goooood* "Okie" food, everything—even cigarettes and snuff were provided for them. Chiropractors, haircuts, and medical needs were also provided.

We aren't surprised because we know "Okie Spirit," but it was a welcome surprise for them.

∞

***Holly J. Schaeffer is an American Red Cross
volunteer who was assigned a variety of tasks.***

The three B's of an Oklahoma disaster are: beef jerky,
bubble gum, and bottled water.

One of the errands I helped with on the third day after
the bombing was transporting dog food to the scene. The
rescue dogs were each in need of the brand of food that they
would normally eat. Otherwise, they risked getting sick due
to a change of diet.

∞

***Cheryl Sing worked as an American Red Cross
volunteer, helping with clerical needs at the
Command Center and on-site food services.***

We came to a small town that had been set up in a parking garage. We started serving a very hearty Oklahoma
breakfast. A young rescuer from California was in line and I
overheard him talking to his friend. "I've been here eight
days, worked my butt off, and gained eight pounds. These
people know how to cook." I smiled and told him, "Your
mother couldn't be here, so we are. Be sure and get some
fruit."

On another day I bumped into a young airman from
Tinker Air Force Base who was on his way to a well-deserved
break. He had a soda and a package of chips in his hand. I
heard the chips crunching. "Excuse me," I said.

He replied, "That's okay, ma'am, I'm in camouflage."

I replied, "It worked!" What a wonderful young man.

∞

***Mick Hinton is a reporter for the* Daily Oklaho-
man. *He accompanied Governor Frank Keating
for a day during the week after the bombing.***

After the governor greeted the entire Dallas Cowboys football team at the downtown Myriad Convention Center, he happened by me and said, "Where's Emmitt? Have you seen him?" The governor was referring to Emmitt Smith, running back for the Cowboys. I got a kick out of that; the governor, too, has his heroes.

The Governor and his wife had gone to the Medical Examiner's office to deliver roses to the workers. "They've had such a tough, tough time examining the bodies," he said. "Cathy and I gave each one of them a rose," so they would have something living in the midst of all that death.

Journalists, like myself, hesitate to call anyone a hero, but the governor certainly performed a heroic role during these worst of times for Oklahoma City.

∽

Jerry Bower is a captain with the Del City, Oklahoma, Fire Department.

On Friday, April 23, I returned to the site as part of a four-man search and rescue crew assigned to the Athenian Restaurant Building. The rescue dogs had hit on four victims in this building, and it was our job to find the bodies and bring them out. Our bunker gear made us hot, our safety glasses fogged over constantly, and our respirators were uncomfortable. The building didn't cooperate, either. Piping, glass, wiring, and concrete chunks shifted and slid with each step we took.

When we found the first victim, she was still at her desk. We recovered her body and went to the decontamination area prior to going off duty. We had found only one of the four victims on that first try. It was comforting to know that at least one more was out, that her family could at last say good-bye.

For the next several days I worked on the pile at the front of the Murrah Building. It was a place where bodies were being found on a regular basis. The only way I was able to make it through this period was to keep my mind focused on the job and keep it off the victims.

One evening I sat and talked about it all with my wife. It helped to have someone who really listens, but I wonder when the real healing will start. Sometimes I wonder *if* it will start. I find myself crying a lot easier now. In church the other day they sang "God Bless America," and I cried like a baby.

∞

Major Harvey F. Harwell is Arkansas area commander for the Salvation Army.

A fireman, covered with debris and weary from his grueling task, sat down beside me with his head in his hands. Wanting to help, I asked him if everything was all right. He said, "No, everything is not all right." Yet, he continued on . . . hope strengthening him as he worked.

There was a tenderness in the strong arms of the volunteers. A request came in that had not been asked for in other disasters: American flags to enshroud the bodies of the military victims. They were not brought out until there was a flag to honor them.

∞

David D. Martin is a medical technologist and a volunteer for the American Red Cross.

I answered the phones at the First Christian Church office for several days. I talked to people from every part of this great nation. It was a very emotional job, to learn that this country is still full of loving and caring people.

I talked to Connecticut social workers who were sending money for the children. From California a company sent angel pins for the volunteers. A church worker from Jacksonville, Florida, called wanting to send toys for the chil-

190

dren. The Hard Rock Cafe in Los Angeles informed us they were donating their entire sales from May 3. Louisiana State Troopers promised to send money for Baylee Almon's family. A woman called from Columbus to offer money and told me she had read in the newspaper that people all over town were having garage sales to raise money to send.

From Nashville, Tennessee, a teacher called to announce cards made for the rescuers were being sent by her elementary school. She asked, "I don't have much money, but what else can I do to help?" This is what it was like from New Mexico, Minnesota, Virginia, Indiana, North Carolina, Illinois, New York, Texas, Iowa, Mississippi, Georgia, and of course, Oklahoma.

As my minister, Don Alexander of the First Christian Church of Oklahoma City, said, "Tragedy does not produce goodness, but it will often reveal it."

∞

Ladonna Harris heard the explosion at her work place in far western Oklahoma City. Her sister, Linda "Coleen" Housley, worked in the Murrah Building.

I started calling all the hospitals. She was not at any of them. I called the Red Cross, but could not get through. I tried for hours. I watched the TV in our break room at lunch time, not wanting to believe this had really happened. I finally left work forty-five minutes before my shift ended. I could not stand it anymore. I had to do something. We took pictures of Coleen to the First Christian Church so they could give one to the Medical Examiner's Office along with descriptions of what she was wearing, what she looked like, and even what her wedding rings looked like. We took pictures to every hospital.

I watched the news day and night. There was no sleep.
Day 1: Hoping and praying for a miracle. No word.

Day 4: Hoping and praying for a miracle. No word. Getting more depressed. Co-workers brought food for us.

Day 6: Very little hope. Prayers weren't helping. Too many memories and tears. No word.

Day 7: I sat on the sofa and cried all day. I did not even get dressed. I felt helpless. Hope fading. No word.

Day 10: My husband made me get out of the house. He took me for a ride. I had not been out of the house for five days. No word.

Day 12: Still more waiting. Hope diminished. Having bad dreams day and night. Was she in one piece? Couldn't get it out of my mind. No word.

Day 13: The day we had been waiting for, but dreaded. We were relieved at the same time. We went to the church on Walker. The Medical Examiner was there, and a nice woman from the Salvation Army. We received the news: Coleen was dead. "Positive identification," they said. I still had doubts. They would not tell us where they found her, or if she was "all there." "It's a crime scene," they kept saying. I called the funeral home. They would pick up Coleen's body that evening.

Day 14: Went to the funeral home. Made arrangements and picked out a casket—the hardest thing I ever had to do. I was finally told she was "all there" and that she died instantly. I can only hope they are right. I still wanted to believe that it was not her, that she was walking around somewhere, not knowing who she was. They brought out her personal belongings: wedding rings, mother's ring, etc. I realized it must really be her body in the casket. More tears than ever before.

Day 15: Day before the funeral. So many things to do, so many people to call. Would it ever be over? Too many tears. My mind still going wild.

Day 16: The final day arrived. There were approximately 800 people at the funeral. More flowers than I could imagine. I think Coleen was looking down from heaven in awe. The service was the nicest I had ever been to or could hope for anyone. We went to the cemetery to lay her to rest not far from our parents. So many people mourned. Such a waste of so many lives.

I have so many memories of Coleen and me as children. I am grateful for that. It's not the same as having her around, but I guess it will have to do.

∞

Army Sergeant Kenneth Ramsby is assigned to Bravo Battery, Personnel and Support Battalion at Fort Sill, Oklahoma.

Once I was sent to an apartment building that had been damaged by the blast. I was to retrieve records that might help identify victims and get any documents (wills, insurance policies, etc.) that might assist the family members. Later, my commander asked me to return to the building, as the mother of one of the victims wanted us to find a stuffed bear she hoped to keep as a memento of her son. I found a stuffed bear dressed in a Marine's dress blue uniform and also a brown teddy bear, that was scraggly from being clutched by someone since childhood. There were some other teddy bears as well. To make sure the mother got her wish, I collected all of them for her. I suspect that the brown scraggly one was the one she wanted.

∞

Carla Garrett was the aunt of two-year-old Tevin Garrett, who died in the explosion.

As I watched the news on TV other employees gathered in our office to see what had happened. I saw terrible things on the screen, then suddenly I saw something that made me scream. "That's my sister!" I yelled. "Look, that's my sister!" People in the room were saying, "Well, she's all right then since we saw her on TV."

I said, "No, she isn't. Her son is in the Federal Building's daycare center." The news reported that some children had been taken to various hospitals. My friend Joan and I went first to Children's Hospital to look for my sister and her little boy. Hospital staff were really helpful in letting us use their phones and offices while we waited to hear any news.

As I waited with Joan, there was a report of an unidentified little boy who had been taken to Presbyterian Hospital. As we left, I heard a young woman sobbing and saw it was my sister. She jumped up and ran over to me. As we hugged each other she said, "I can't find Tevin, my little baby." I told her that my friend and I were going to Presbyterian to see if the unidentified child was hers.

My sister went to St. Anthony, which is where Joan and I ended up after leaving Presbyterian. St. Anthony had a disaster center set up for the families, where there were many lists of people who were injured and being treated. My little nephew's name was not on any of the lists. Later that night, we were told to go to the First Christian Church for further information.

Several days later, the medical examiner broke down in tears while talking to the families about going to our homes to collect personal items to help them identify our loved ones. I knew this wasn't good news, but I kept the faith until they identified Tevin as being one of the children who died on the second floor in the daycare.

The governor of Illinois, my home state, sent donated teddy bears to Oklahoma. They were passed out at the prayer service attended by President Clinton.

∽

Edye Smith's two sons, Chase, 3, and Colton, 2, were both killed in the bombing.

I had just completed the purchase of my house the day before the bombing, and the kids ran through it. Chase said,

Left:
A personal tribute to a child victim is displayed at the bomb site memorial.
— **Photo courtesy of Barry Shisler**

Below:
Canteens such as this provided hot food to rescuers and volunteers around the clock.
— **Photo courtesy of Lee Brouwer**

"Is this going to be *our* house? Mommy, Uncle Danny, Papa, Nana, Uncle Bart and Uncle Matte . . . we're all going to live here?"

"No, just you, me and Colton," I said.

The next morning started as a normal day for us. We got in my Jeep to go to work, and Chase kept kicking the back of my seat. When we got to the daycare, Chase took off his seat belt and jumped out of the car. Colton wanted me to hold him and carry him.

We went up the elevator to the daycare. Chase went to sit on the floor with his friends, while I tried to kiss Colton. He pretended not to want a kiss. I made a sad face and said, "Boo hoo." He gave me a kiss and hug. I went to Chase on the floor, and he hugged me so that he could get back to playing. I signed them in, and that's the last time I saw them alive.

My office was getting ready to have a birthday party for me when we heard the explosion. We looked out the windows, and all we could see was black smoke.

My mother came down to my office, and when we went outside, we could hear glass landing on the sidewalk.

Then Mom said, "Oh, my God, the babies."

That's when we ran up the street. I kept saying, "You don't think it was the building the babies are in, do you? You don't think anyone would bomb that building, do you?"

She said, "No, everything is going to be OK."

We ran toward the back of the building, so we didn't really know until we crossed the street that it was the building that had been bombed. Within five minutes they were pushing people back. We asked everyone where my children were. The other two daycare centers in the area had been evacuated. We stayed there a couple of hours, waiting. Finally, someone told us to go to Children's Hospital, that some of the babies had been taken there.

I knew from the very moment I looked at that building that my children were dead. I was just waiting for someone to come and tell me. The staff at the hospital came out every once in a while with a list of survivors and called out names. They always went right past Smith.

My brother, Daniel Coss, who is a police officer, went back to the playground to look for Chase and Colton. Off to the side he saw one child wrapped up on a bench. That's the first child he went to. It was Colton. The other police officer there tried to get him to go home. Then Presbyterian announced they had an unidentified three-year-old. Daniel went there next and called me to ask what Chase had been wearing, but the clothing didn't match. It wasn't Chase. That was the one time we held out real hope. Then my brother found Chase's body at the Medical Examiner's.

I was raised in a Christian home, and I know that my kids are in heaven. Their bodies are in the grave, but they are in heaven. That's what keeps me going. At night time it's really hard. That's when I wonder, "Why did this happen?" I know they're better off, but it still doesn't ease the pain.

We watched the home videos and have been able to laugh at the funny things they did. They had outrageous senses of humor. Both my boys weighed right at 45 pounds and they were almost two years apart. Colton, the youngest, ate everything. People called him "fat rat" and "chunky monkey."

One time we couldn't find him and began looking everywhere, including the neighbor's house and in the garage. I decided to check the bedroom and heard a munching sound. I looked under the bed first, then realized the sound was coming from the closet. There was Colton, eating a plastic candy cane full of Reese's Peanut butter cups. He had chocolate all over his face, as well as his clothes and the carpet.

Chase was very courteous. He would open doors for women and say, "Here you go, pretty lady." All the ladies loved him. He received a certificate from the daycare for being such a good helper. The boys were so close. Chase watched out for Colton. He wanted to take care of his little brother.

Life's never going to be the same. We will never know life as we used to, but knowing that my kids are in heaven and that I'll see then again someday brings me a lot of peace. I'm going to go on with my life for them.

ഇ

Captain D. Paul Fuller is a disaster social service coordinator for the Salvation Army.

During the first few hours I talked with everyone from search dog handlers to FBI and ATF agents, from construction workers to Air Force generals, but none of those had the impact that one Secret Service Agent had on my life.

Outfitted in a jumpsuit and wearing protective gloves, mask, and goggles, this agent, identified by his bright yellow vest, approached our canteen. A simple request was his first statement, as I offered him something cold to drink.

"Do you have a Zip-loc sandwich bag?" the tired young man asked.

"I don't know, but I will look," I replied. I found one and handed it to a volunteer who was helping. I stood close by and watched as the canteen helper opened the bag and held it out. The agent then removed a badge and ID wallet from his vest pocket and placed it securely within the Zip-loc container. I could only guess what emotions the agent was feeling. The recovered ID and badge——did they belong to a friend, a partner, a fellow officer?

As the agent placed the items within the bag, a silence fell over the three of us. It seemed as if each one of us were sealing that bag with hope and a prayer.

ഇ

Susie Malone is an American Red Cross volunteer who helped care for the children of the families as they waited for news of missing loved ones.

When I arrived at the First Christian Church, everything looked normal except for the children. They were quiet and seemed to be somewhat numb.

I looked into one young boy's eyes. It was like looking at glass—no expression, no emotion. One little girl named Alyssa caught my attention. She came right up to me and asked me to help her paint, get toys, and then get something to eat and drink. Her feelings went from one extreme to the other. She wanted to be happy and play, but the sadness wouldn't let her. The children knew full well the seriousness of the tragedy in spite of their ages.

∞

Sara Williams is a student at Oklahoma State University. She submitted this column to the school's newspaper, while her father, W. Stephen Williams, was still missing.

You're right, Dad. You told me that I was too impatient at times. I really never thought that I would ever have to test my patience to the degree that I am now.

It has now been 96 hours since I first learned of this madness. My life has never hinged upon a phone call as it is right now.

This whole scenario brings to mind the sermon by Jonathon Edwards, "Sinners in the Hands of an Angry God." One ring could lurch my spirits and those of my entire family into the depths of hell.

I keep expecting you to walk in the door and join Mom and me for your weekly Sunday morning before-church routine.

I am not home often, but when I am, you can be sure that you and Mom and I can be found contemplating topics discussed on "This Week." You are always encouraging Sam Donaldson and Cokie Roberts, your two political comrades-in-spirit.

I remember the time I gave kudos to George Will for one of his statements on some controversial issue. You said, "Sara, can't you see, you are too far right!"

"Oh, you yellow dog Democrat," I muttered under my breath.

It was all in good fun, but I'm thankful that you have allowed me to develop my views, even though at times they have been a bit different from your own.

You didn't allow me to merely think like you thought. You invited me—urged me, really—to think for myself. Every time I expressed an opinion, you didn't ask me why I didn't think like you did. You asked me why I thought like I did.

Thank you for that. Thanks for the challenge.

You know what, Dad? I always tell everyone how sorry I feel for you because you have three daughters and no sons. Four women can really dish out a lot, especially with our family's genes! But all this time, I have really not been sorry at all. If you had had a son, we might not have climbed Mt. Princeton together, or gone hunting and fishing together, or have ridden the Shockwave at Six Flags five times in a row, or built that picnic table from hell. You remember the one. We must have used that silly level about 3,000 times, and it still never came out just exactly right!

I think we both decided that something was seriously wrong with that level. I mean, how could it have been faulty Williams engineering?

I guess if you had had a son, he would automatically have been stuck with the task of lawn mowing. Instead, you had to attempt to bribe me to do it. Do you remember?

"Sara, if you mow the lawn every weekend this summer, I will give you the keys to a brand new Honda."

"What's the catch?"

"No catch."

"Can I get it in writing?"

"Of course," you said with a serious look. We shook on it.

"Now go look out back."

I jumped up from the couch and peered out the back door. A lawnmower—a brand new Honda lawnmower. Not a good way to get the summer started. Of course, you thought so.

Mom reprimanded you on my behalf.

"Steve, that's not very nice." You laughed and laughed. I still have never touched that lawnmower.

Dad, thanks for all the little things you have done.

Thanks for answering all my hundreds of questions when Meryl was born.

Thank you for telling me the difference between a square and a rectangle.

Thanks for stopping what you were doing at work every time I called to brag about my ACT score or a test grade or my first four-point in college.

I remember my senior year in high school, when I got the letter in the mail about the scholarship to OSU. I rushed right in the house and called you immediately. You probably drove everyone at your office crazy bragging about me.

Remember Dad's Day, 1991, when I was a freshman? You weren't really sure at this point what to think about the whole "Theta" thing, but we had a lot of fun.

Over the past four years you have seen Theta become a significant part of my life.

We hosted the Eddie Sutton Show at the house once and you called in to ask a question. But before you did, you said "Hi" to me, because I was in the audience. All my Theta sisters thought that was the coolest thing! I was so embarrassed, but secretly I loved it.

On November 7, 1993, I was slated to become the chapter president. Who do you think was the first person I called? Dad, you were so proud of me. I remember seeing some of your friends after I was slated, and they all congratulated me: "Your dad is so proud."

Dad, I'm sorry that I never went to play golf with you.

I'm sorry that almost every time you pulled out your guitar to play, I asked you to be quiet because I couldn't hear the television.

I'm sorry that I didn't volunteer to help you mow the yard every weekend or pull weeds or plant the garden.

I'm sorry that I haven't called you every day since I've been at college just to tell you that I love you and that I was thinking about you.

I'm sorry that I drank all the milk when I was at home on the weekend.

I'm sorry that Allyson, Meryl, and I dog-piled you, while Mom tickled your feet. Wait, maybe I'm not sorry about that. That was pretty funny.

I'm really sorry that I ever told you I might go to the University of Oklahoma. You never said it, but I know that the very thought of me in the midst of the "tea sippers" in Norman tormented you. The doctors wouldn't confirm it, but we both know you have orange blood running through those veins of yours. When you found out that I would be attending your alma mater, you were so excited. We even sang the alma mater together at one of the football games this year.

Dad, please know that I love you with all my heart.

You have satisfied more roles in my life than the average "father" ever thought about. I always watch you, even when you don't know it, and I see the little things that make you special.

I hope that wherever you are you will be home soon. I hope that you aren't cold or sad or hungry.

I keep thinking that this is about some other people and I just know that at any time you are going to walk through the back door and I am going to say, "Dad, can you believe what is happening in this world?"

I would give anything if you would just open that door right now, grinning that boyish grin with your Ray Bans on and golf clubs thrown over your shoulder, bragging about your latest great day on the course.

I would give anything if I could go out in the garage and hear you strumming up a little "Wonderful Tonight" by Eric Clapton.

I miss you, Dad. Please come home.

*Major David A. Wiist is a fire prevention
specialist and fire investigator with the
Edmond, Oklahoma, Fire Department.*

When our turn finally came, we were sent to the entry
point on NW 5th, where we "geared up" with goggles, knee
and elbow pads, and respirators. A division leader explained
exactly what we were to do, including two statements that
were repeated often: "Don't talk to the press," and "Don't
take cameras with you."

Once inside the fence, our first job was to move a thirty-
foot steel pipe toward the basement for use in shoring up
the building. Collapse, at this point, was constantly in our
minds.

A few hours after our first assignment we were sent to
what was now known as the "pit," where we assisted a FEMA
rescue team from Virginia Beach. We removed debris by the
bucket load, working in unison like a human chain. Files,
telephones, computers, purses, pens, shoes, clothing, furniture, everything you'd expect to find in an office building
was mixed in the rubble, crushed by slabs of concrete as big
as fire trucks. We'd dig as far as we could with our hands,
then call in cutting torches or cranes for the more massive
pieces of concrete and steel. All around I watched other
teams doing the same thing.

∽

*Charles Rountree is a life insurance agent who
worked the midnight shift at a Salvation Army
canteen.*

My Salvation Army canteen cart was right across the
street from where the Ryder truck was parked. This area was
"my neighborhood." I've been coming downtown every day
around 5:00 P.M. to swim and steam at the YMCA for fifteen
years, Monday through Friday.

At first I was assigned to canteen duty in the outer perimeter. That first night two rescue workers from Metro Dade County, Florida, crawled out of the pit and came over for hot food. We asked them if there was anything we could do for them, and after much hemming and hawing, they sheepishly admitted they had a flag football team, but they hadn't been able to practice, since they had no football. I told them to have a seat and enjoy their dinner. My co-worker got on her ham radio and called the Salvation Army command center fifteen blocks south and made a request. Twenty minutes later a van pulled up to our canteen with the two footballs.

On the night of April 30, I went into the pit for a twelve-hour shift with a liquid canteen cart. I had to get a tetanus shot, wear protective rubber gloves, and get the "color of the day"—a bright orange dot—pasted on my ID tag. Two Salvation Army volunteers were the only civilians in the pit that night.

When the Puget Sound, Washington, Fire and Rescue Squad completed their last shift, they prepared to head for home. Suddenly, right next to our canteen, they formed into ranks with a flag bearer at the front. It was just like Team USA marching in at the Olympics. They marched up to the rubble and planted the flag. After a moment of silence, the formation turned and made its way out. As the team was coming up a slight rise, I instinctively gave two thumbs up and every team member returned my salute. It began to thunder and lightning, and a sharp cold rain started to fall.

We were crying and I found myself embracing two of these big burly guys. One of them looked me right in the eye and said, "You people didn't deserve this. God bless you and God bless Oklahoma City."

∽

Debbie Drain works for the Oklahoma Department of Human Services.

Above: An abundance of food, all donated, was ever-present throughout the search operation.
— **Photo courtesy of Lee Brouwer**

Below: Construction cranes worked twenty-four hours a day to prevent additional collapse. — **Photo courtesy of Oscar Johnson**

The first day I was there was on Wednesday, May 3. A rescue worker came in to get some alcohol and a bandage for his finger. While I was cleaning the wound and applying a bandage, he started talking. He told me that he was only a construction worker and just happened to be in the area at the time of the blast. He then said he had been one of the first to arrive and gave me details about the rescue of survivors and about pulling out bodies of babies. I was not prepared for that, yet I stood there, listening. About two hours later he came back, looking for some gloves. He seemed to zero in on me and started talking again. I felt compelled to listen. I think in some way I was helping him just by listening.

I also helped make bandannas for the rescuers. Lisa Love was responsible for starting this project. Some of the guys came in asking for bandannas to cover their faces while working in the building. Lisa had some flag material and made a couple of bandannas for them. That few turned into hundreds.

At the memorial service for the rescuers, I saw many police officers wearing the bandannas around their necks, tucked neatly under the collars of their uniforms. They looked so sharp and so proud! That gave me such a warm, satisfying, and patriotic feeling!

∽

Sharlotte Campbell and her nine-month-old spider monkey, Charlie, volunteered their time and services at the Family Center in the First Christian Church.

When we saw the children, we were surprised to see a dozen or so sitting quietly, holding toys. They were not playing with each other, and an unnatural silence covered their area of the room. Then the children looked up and saw Charlie. They jumped to their feet yelling, "Monkey! Monkey! Monkey!" Laughter and giggles could be heard throughout the large room. The adults looked our way to see what

206

was happening, and when they saw Charlie playing in his monkey ways, they too started pointing and smiling. The children had their pictures taken one by one with Charlie. Then the pictures were given to them—a little joy in their hands to show to others.

Charlie was asked to go to the home of a four-year-old little girl. Her mother had said the child's best friend was her father and that he was one of the missing. The little girl had not eaten food, other than juice and water, from Wednesday through Saturday. As I entered the room, the little girl became immediately excited when she saw Charlie in my arms, and she ran across the room saying, "Monkey! Monkey!"

Charlie and I were at the bombing site when family members were allowed for the first time to pass in front of the Federal Building and see the destruction that had taken place. Charlie and I walked several family members through, and once again Charlie gave out hugs, handshakes, and desperately needed good humor in the midst of such grief.

∽

Bennie Thomas is a captain with the Broken Arrow, Oklahoma, Fire Department.

After processing through, we heard that family members wanted all the firefighters to wear ribbons, when entering the building.

Being the team leader, I went to the main gate and inquired where the ribbons could be obtained. I was told that family members were across the street on the corner of 8th and Harvey, and to see the man in the Razorback T-shirt.

After crossing the street, I introduced myself as a firefighter from Broken Arrow. I was overwhelmed by the praise and appreciation they had for the rescue workers involved. I was told that the wife of the man in the Razorback T-shirt was missing. Looking at him, I could see the hurt, frustration, and fatigue on his face, and I felt my throat swell and the tears welling up. I couldn't look him in the eyes. He asked if he could pin on my guardian angel ribbon so I would have someone watching over me. I said "yes," thanked him, and assured him that he would be in my prayers.

Later, my thoughts returned to the family members and to the man in the T-shirt. I could not help but wonder if we had brought his wait to an end or if it must continue another day. And another, and another . . .

∽

Firefighter John Clement of Sacramento, California, is a member of that city's Urban Search and Rescue Team.

Late in our first shift we were crawling through a tunnel that was later called the "cave." It was in the basement area where the last floor had pinned a dozen or more bodies in a space we could barely squeeze through. It was just myself and one other rescuer freeing the bodies one by one. There was no room for other rescuers. We handed debris back out of the hole in a chain of firefighters. I couldn't stop thinking about the huge mass of broken concrete over our heads. Nine floors of concrete slabs compressed, held together only by rebar. What if it shifted? If it settled?

As we cleared debris from the bodies, we could see additional victims deeper in the hole. The Chaplain wasn't kidding when he had said it was bad. He had tried to prepare us for the carnage we were about to witness, but I had no idea it would be like this. It didn't really hit home until I found an identification on the body I was digging out. I looked at the driver's license picture and saw a real human being. She was around my age. I'm sure she had dreams and ambitions much the same as mine. I felt terrible for her—there she was, gone, a pile of concrete and flesh. It didn't seem real, the bodies; they looked like bloodied dolls stacked on top of one another, entwined with the dirty, jagged concrete and steel.

Carol Kitchen is a computer analyst at Tinker Air Force Base.

I knew four of the victims personally, but the scene I remember most was at the funeral for one of them. The victim and her husband had both been Army Recruiters, and they had five children. At the funeral there were uniforms in abundance: Army, Cub Scouts, and Boy Scouts. The couple had also been Scout Leaders. I will never forget the father sitting on the front row at the funeral with his five children. Eventually, he crawled down on the floor in front of the kids so he could console all five at one time.

∽

Bobbie Cole, whose office was downtown, volunteered to help any way she could.

I assisted about thirty men in finding raincoats. I think it was the Sheriff from El Reno who best represented the spirit of camaraderie at the command post. He took off work to help his friends and neighbors, relying on his own people to take up the slack back home.

Late one evening, after his tour in the trenches was complete, he took off the raincoat and offered it to me, even though he knew he'd be back the following day.

"Give it to one of the new boys," he said quietly. "They'll be needing it more than I will tonight." With that, he left, braving the rain without a wrap as he headed for his own vehicle.

Every soul I met seemed linked and synchronized—every deputy, commanding officer, and public servant volunteer. They made me feel safe. It suddenly didn't matter that there were other bomb threats or that my son and I had been so close to the building when it exploded. These men and women placed others before themselves. They truly valued life, but they were willing to risk their own lives to help. So, when the front line workers needed flashlights, batteries, raincoats, and coffee, the choice was easy to make. I went. I've never regretted a frightening, soggy minute of it.

∾

Major Roy C. Tolcher is the commanding officer for the Big Spring, Texas, Corps of the Salvation Army.

One young fireman came to our canteen for some refreshment. I noticed he seemed to be talking to himself. As he got closer, the words that came out were, "I found one. I found one. I found one." Being able to be some comfort, I assured this young man that he had just helped a family have some peace. Over and over again, I witnessed men with weariness go again into the "pit" with hope that they would be able to find someone alive, somehow knowing in my own heart that it was virtually impossible, but there was always that hope.

∾

Dr. Jim Clark, a dentist from Ada, Oklahoma, is a member of the Oklahoma Air National Guard.

Although I have been trained in forensic dentistry, I was not ready for what I would experience. To work in a room with so many doctors—MD's, PhD's, and DDS's—and not have a bunch of egos to deal with was an unusual event. We cried, we laughed, but most of all we were proud of the job we did. We placed those victims back with their families very quickly. My hat is off to the funeral directors who stayed with every victim through the whole process. The second day I was there I saw my old neuro-anatomy professor,

210

Dr. Roberts, sweeping the floor and taking out the trash. Everyone was there to do whatever they could to help. The support was unbelievable. Hot food was served three times a day. Ice cream, sodas and snacks were there anytime we wanted them. One highlight of a bad time was when I met Dr. Red Duke. He came by to shake hands and slap everyone on the back for a job well done. It helped.

∞

Eddie Binyon is a FEMA-trained funeral director from Chickasha, Oklahoma.

For hours we heard story after heart-wrenching story. Families had lost children. They stood before us in a daze. I remember two young men reporting their mother missing. They looked so empty. Family after family gave the reports: name, age, sex, height, and weight. We asked about scars, surgeries, tattoos, previous broken bones, color of eyes and hair. "Can you tell me what they had on today?" It was a question asked time and again. Sometimes they had a response; sometimes there was no answer.

The questions became more difficult for many. What was their doctor's name? Who was their dentist? Then came the explanation of the search and recovery process. We could only assure them that everyone in the building would be found. At that point it was still hoped some would be alive. Somewhere around 300 people were reported missing.

Strangely enough, the last family I interviewed was also from my community, someone I knew well. It broke my heart to ask these questions of them.

More heartache came my way in the days to come. I watched for those I knew. Each was found only after time and agony had gone by. Embalmers and funeral directors were divided in groups. My assignment for most of the sixteen days involved identification. We were the ones who notified the assistance center when a body had been positively identified. No one could be too careful. We could not

211

make mistakes! Another group was used to follow a body through the examination and data collection process. People with careers in the funeral profession were seeing things indescribable, things they will remember the rest of their lives. The last group was stationed at the Family Assistance Center, where they answered questions from the families and performed the difficult task of official notification of the next of kin.

At the Medical Examiner's Office, information collected was put into a data base. Called *ante*mortem information, it was carefully put into categories so it could be matched to *post*mortem records. As the postmortem records were entered, the data base was matched to the antemortem records. When a possible match was made, dental records or fingerprints could be used to make the identification official.

I remember the first body I saw in the morgue. There lay a sweet child, a child in a condition different than any child I had seen in twenty years of funeral service. The mood in the room was a quiet, busy rush, as all had much work to do. Everyone was seeing things they had never seen before. Body after body was taken through the steps necessary to make a biological identification. X-rays were taken, followed by photographs and fingerprints. Doctors made examinations and documented everything they observed. Then the dental teams took over.

Those found first were killed by the bomb. Victims killed by the building were found after a few days. There was a distinct difference. Most of the people found after April 22 were intact, killed by blows to the head or chest. Families were anxious. After a few days, they were begging to have them found even if they were dead. It seemed strange to see them wait for bad news in order to feel better, but that was the case. Virtually every death certificate showed the same thing: "Cause of death: multiple injuries; homicide; bombing. Time of death: 9:04 A.M., April 19, 1995."

Friday, May 6, was our last day. Everyone had been found but two women and one man who would be added later. Three of the babies found would require DNA tests to be identified.

At first it took a few days for America to understand the difficult jobs the workers were doing, but then the support began to flow from across our land. It was felt. It was strong. Power was among us. Our people have stood proud during this time, and we are all thankful to those who donated time, money, and prayers for the volunteers. They have been valiant.

∞

Cynthia M. DeMarco worked the night shift at a Salvation Army canteen.

The east side of the building was also the location of the morgue, set up in the basement of the First Methodist Church. The two 18-wheeled refrigerated trailers parked at the entrance were a somber and constant reminder of what was going on. I found it ironic, when gazing up at the church, there remained among the destruction a banner hanging just above the entrance to the morgue that read: "Mind, Body and Spirit Preschool. For Information Call. . ."

∞

Lynn Butts Preston of Boulder, Colorado, is the stepsister of Housing and Urban Development employee Betsy McGonnell.

I did not hear about the bombing on April 19 until I was driving to meet some friends for lunch. I turned on the radio and heard brief mention of it. After lunch I listened again, and realized its magnitude was much greater than I had first thought. I drove home and flipped on the TV. My phone began ringing. I started to cry and felt sick. My stepmother's only child, Betsy McGonnell, was one of the victims.

I tried all day to get through on the phone, but couldn't. Then Melissa, my sister in Oklahoma City, reached me later that night only to report that Betsy still had not been found. A command post for families had been set up at the First Christian Church in Oklahoma City. Melissa said she was asked to provide Betsy's Social Security number, dental records, and a description of what she had worn to work that morning.

I came to Oklahoma City with a friend who had a son at the University of Tulsa. As we drove into the city we saw that all the flags were at half mast. She drove me to my parents' house.

Mary, my stepmother, stayed up one night and wrote Betsy's obituary. She asked me to help her with the corrections. Then Betsy's daughter, Jamie, took it to the newspaper. Mary said Jamie had been a rock throughout this ordeal.

While I was there, Mary held up well until we went to see the ruins of the building with the other families on May 6. The first thing Mary and I saw when we got off the bus was a traffic signal that had been knocked askew by the blast. Then we saw the old Methodist church, that was across the street from the Federal Building. Its windows were out and parts of the building were gone. I looked at its sign in front, which still held part of its Easter Sunday message.

At first we looked at the building from a distance. It was a sight so much more powerful than any of the pictures we had seen on television. The fact that Betsy's body had been found on the ground level illustrated to us for the first time what had happened to the victims when the bomb went off. They had poured through the opening and down . . . down to the ground.

Mary fell apart, and, finally, Jamie did too. We all cried. An FBI chaplain put his arms around me, and another chaplain put his arms around Mary. They even called us by name.

ℭℴℴ

Captain Edward Alonzo is a commanding officer with the Salvation Army. He worked at the site as well as in the counseling center.

214

Above: This slab of concrete, once it was inscribed, became a gathering place for flowers and other sentiments. **— Photo courtesy of Barry Shisler**

Below: One of several memorial services held in the street in front of the Federal Building. **— Photo courtesy of Barry Shisler**

215

The mother who lost her four-year-old daughter was doing a television interview. I could tell she was angry. She said on television, "I don't understand how anybody could kill innocent children." I was there waiting for the interview to be over in order to present her two other children with teddy bears. As the interview ended, I approached the mother and asked if she would allow us to give the teddy bears to her surviving children. She was very receptive and said, "Sure." She noticed I was from Texas and immediately expressed her gratitude. She said, "I appreciate your help and your leaving your family to come here and help us." I told her we were here to serve in any capacity in providing relief and rescue. I expressed to her that we would uphold her and her family in our prayers. She said, "Thank you."

I asked her how she was doing and she said, "At first I was angry that I lost my little girl. Then I thought I was being selfish. I figured God needed little angels to hug, kiss, and play with in heaven. I believe my child is now an angel in heaven and is being looked after by God." I expressed to her that she was correct.

ᝡ

Mrs. Dixie VanEss, wife of HUD victim John Karl VanEss, penned these thoughts with her daughters, Kevin and Kerry, and sons, Karl and Dan.

We always will be haunted by the fact that we heard and felt the moment that John died. A sound that we first thought was a sonic boom changed our lives forever.

A phone call from a family friend shortly afterward was our first notification that a bomb had gone off in downtown Oklahoma City. Kerry, who was watching the live coverage on TV, almost fainted when she recognized it as Dad's office building. She knew his office was on the seventh floor and that his desk was on the north side, right in front of the windows. That whole area was gone.

Karl and Dan left work and started hunting, hospital to hospital. We received some conflicting reports that John had been seen alive in one of the hospitals. We even thought we saw him on television on a stretcher.

Our only thought during the ride from Chickasha, Oklahoma, to Oklahoma City was, "It doesn't matter what condition John is in. He's alive and we're going to take care of him." When she reached the hospital, no one could locate John, so we waited with other families for the news.

For six days we waited. All the days began to run together. The first day or two we were eager to hear the phone ring, but as the days went on we had to have someone come over to answer the phone for us. It was like having a six-day funeral. Every night when we went to bed or tried to eat we felt guilty. We thought about John being cold, hurt or hungry. When we finally received the news that John's body had been found, it was a relief.

∞

Anthony and Beth Cooper lost their daughter-in-law, Dana, and grandson, Christopher, on April 19.

I tried to call the day care center where Dana worked, and the line was busy. I called Beth and told her we had to go downtown, that there had been an explosion. Then I called our son, A. C., and told him. He said he would meet us there.

The closest we could park was at 3rd and Broadway. As we walked to the Federal Building, there was glass everywhere, windows missing, doors gone. You could see cracks in the buildings and sidewalks. Everywhere you looked there was damage.

Dana was the new director of the day care at the Federal Building, and we were all very proud of her. Christopher went to the day care with her. Dana loved kids. She loved to care for them, teach, and protect them. Dana said she had

217

the best of both worlds: a job she loved and one where she could still be with Christopher.

Anthony Christopher Cooper II. We called him Christopher. He was two and a half years old, and from the eyes of first-time grandparents, this little cotton-headed boy could do no wrong. We watched him every Wednesday so Dana could attend school to get her degree to teach kindergarten or first grade. Grandma spoiled him a little each week and sent him home to his mother and daddy. Beth said that is what grandmothers are supposed to do, and she was very good at it.

They were not found that day. Like many others, we watched the television in hope of a miracle, but it never came. On April 22 we were notified that Christopher had been identified, and on April 23 we were told that Dana had been found. We laid Dana and Christopher to rest on April 26, 1995.

∾

Lieutenant Tom Miner of the Pierce County Sheriff's Department in Tacoma, Washington, is a FEMA Task Force Leader with the Puget Sound Urban Search and Rescue Task Force.

There are many moments that I remember. I was the Plans Section Chief for the night shift, which meant I developed the next shift's action plan based on progress and information gathered during my shift.

The first unforgettable experience occurred on Sunday, April 23, when I was asked to be part of the delegation to meet the President, who was scheduled to attend the Memorial Service at the State Fairgrounds Arena. It was the first time I had been outside the disaster site and among the public since arrival. As we entered the arena, the people in the stands and on the floor saw us walk in and immediately started cheering as we walked across the floor. They gave us a standing ovation that continued even after we were behind the stage. It sent chills up my spine to realize how important we were to these thousands of people.

We spent about forty-five minutes with the President, briefing him on what we were doing and talking about what it was like and what was needed to get the job done. He was silent for several moments, and his eyes watered as he looked at the photos we had brought from inside the building. He then pledged total support for what we were doing and asked us to be careful. He then told us to lead the way into the arena. Again, the crowd erupted when we appeared. It was a wonderful, uplifting moment for all of us. People reached out to touch us and shake our hands as we walked through. One uniformed Marine cried as he shook each of our hands. I thought it a shame that everyone still working at the site could not experience this moment. It was a truly beautiful and inspirational experience. We returned with renewed vigor and determination to see the job at hand finished, so the wonderful people of Oklahoma and the country could bring some closure to this horrible tragedy.

We had heard that Oklahoma wanted each task force to leave a flag from their state on the building in honor of all the states who sent aid, so I told "Search Team 2" that I had a secret mission for them. About fifteen minutes later I looked up at the roof of the building, and smack in the middle on a small protrusion stood our flag, flapping briskly in the wind. Thinking we had outdone the other task forces, we felt pretty proud. Unfortunately, others within the search and rescue system were concerned that we had committed a breech of etiquette by flying our flag higher than the Oklahoma flag. Fearing possible chastisement from irate Oklahomans, I was soon told in no uncertain terms by the FEMA 1st leader to "Get that damn flag down and five minutes ago would not be too soon."

I called our other task force leader. "Find me an Oklahoma flag as soon as possible and don't come back until you have one."

A few minutes later the Assistant Chief, striding with purpose in our direction, looked up at the flag and asked, "What is that?"

The FEMA 1st leader said, "You mean the Washington State Flag?"

The Chief said, "Dang, that's a pretty flag. We've had the media and a lot other people calling and asking about it." He then asked if we could take it down and give it to him for inclusion in a ceremony being planned to thank all of the out-of-state teams.

We felt honored to have been able to represent our state in Oklahoma, and we hope we left a lasting impression of the quality and nature of the people of Washington State. I will always remember the support, pride, and determination of the people of Oklahoma. Hundreds of volunteers kept us going. They fed us, washed our clothes, cut our hair, massaged our sore muscles, and treated us with love and respect.

I will always feel that what we did pales in comparison to what they did for us.

∽

Dena Nobis-Putney is counselor at Comanche County Memorial Hospital.

The thing that touched me the most that day was when the medical examiner came in to make an announcement. He stood there and told everyone that he was doing the best job he could, but that the bodies were hard to identify due to the nature of the injuries sustained in the explosion. He then began to cry. As he stood there on a chair, crying, the families began to applaud him. It touched me so deeply that a medical examiner, whose job it is to simply identify people, would be so affected by this.

∽

Judy Walker's husband, Bob Walker, died in the Murrah Building.

We spent the first few days at home, haunted faces staring at a television screen that replayed the tragedy over and over. We were powerless to do anything else. Greedily, we snatched at any morsel of new information coming over the air waves while waiting for the phone to ring with the news that Bob had been found. We prayed silently that he was trapped but protected under tented slabs of concrete, and that inaction would keep him alive until we could get his daily medication to him.

We slept double on the beds, the sofa bed, a mattress on the floor in Bob's computer room, and the couch in the den. Our three-bedroom house had never been too big for the two of us, even with Bob's office full of computer equipment and various materials associated with his Boy Scouts, Masonic Lodge, and Shriner affiliations.

For several days we stepped gingerly around each other, grabbing the phone on the first ring and gratefully accepting the flowers and food and fruit baskets brought by our neighbors and friends. The shock of it all continued to hold us in its grip. We prayed for Bob's safety and held confidence in his strength of character and will. If anyone could hold on, my Bob could.

Because of frayed nerves and our quest for first-hand information, we all decided to spend our days at the First Christian Church. We arrived each morning before the Medical Examiner's update at 9:30 and stayed until we were told there would be no more notifications that day. We met the families of missing co-workers. Joann, Mike Thompson's wife, with their two young sons, seemed to find a measure of peace there. The boys clutched stuffed animals donated to the center by people wanting to give of themselves. The center became a refuge for us. We were anonymous to others, yet able to reach out to them when we wanted.

We spent some of our time there making ribbons pinned with angels for the search and rescue workers. Sometimes we answered cards and letters sent by school children. The letters were brief and poignant. One letter from a second-grader said, "I hope the people who did this pay big time."

At the center we were insulated from the press and from well-meaning visitors. We were too immersed in our grief to obtain comfort from friends, no matter how much they wished to console. We found comfort only in others who were experiencing the same pain and hope and fearful expectancy. Counselors, assigned for individual families, were called "escorts." They offered a hand or an ear or shoulder without being intrusive or pushy. They had come from all over the United States.

Bob was found on May 2—his mother's and his son's birthday, and the day after my birthday. By then we weren't sure what we had been praying for: his rescue or just that his body be found. We had to know in our minds he could not have survived, not that close to the blast, but our hearts hadn't been ready to let him go. The medical examiner assured us he had died instantly, that he had not suffered at all. This is the only consolation to me.

∽

Craig Shelley is chief of marine operations with the New York Fire Department and a member of FEMA's New York Task Force 1, Urban Search and Rescue.

I heard about the bombing on television. The pictures seemed so distant from my life. Little did I realize that within twenty-four hours I would be at the site. After arrival in Oklahoma City, I was briefed on our mission and shown our area of operations. Entering the block and standing in front of the destruction literally took my breath away. I was not prepared for what I saw.

Operations were conducted at a feverish pace. At times it seemed that I could not continue that pace, but the people of Oklahoma kept me going. Always a kind word or a gentle touch on the arm or the shoulder. What a comfort it was. People who had been directly affected by the bombing were there for us.

✑

Elaine Sawtell is a FEMA canine search specialist assigned to Nebraska Task Force 1. She lives in Springfield, Missouri.

The call came at 5:00 P.M. Sunday evening, April 30, from FEMA officials in Oklahoma City. "California Task Force 5 only has one dog. Can you come?"

It was the call I had been waiting for since the morning of the explosion. Being the closest FEMA-qualified disaster dog team (Springfield, Missouri), I had hoped to be deployed even if my task force in Lincoln, Nebraska, was not. I wanted the opportunity to let my dog do what she is trained to do: locate live victims trapped in rubble.

"Do you want to drive or fly?" We drove five hours through the rain and pulled into Oklahoma City at 11:00 P.M., ready for the 8:00 A.M. shift. My dog, Ditto, and I knew the dog team from Orange County, Deresa Teller and Bella, a border collie. We had met at the FEMA Canine Search Specialist School in Indiana. Even though I had never met the other members of CA-TF5, we felt like a part of the team from the beginning.

Monday morning, May 1, brought my first sight of the building. My first thought was: it's so big. Pictures on television didn't begin to show its immensity.

Our mission was to assist rescue workers only in recovery, not the rescues we would have liked. Ditto and Bella performed well, though, confirming each other's findings through the twisted wreckage of the building's basement.

Wednesday was a day of good-byes for CA-TF5. Ditto, myself, and several task force members, along with the Edmond, Oklahoma, firefighters, went to St. Elizabeth Ann Seton School. Ditto, who loves children as well as grownups, demonstrated some of her skills for the students and sang along with their rollicking rendition of "Oklahoma." The students presented her with a ball cap, a basket of dog treats, and handmade posters, which we will always treasure.

On Thursday, May 4, we watched our new teammates return to California, then turned our attention once again to the Murrah Building. That evening, we made one last confirming sweep for the Oklahoma City Fire Department.

As the last remaining FEMA dog team, FEMA officials asked if we would stay over for the rescue workers' memorial service on Friday afternoon, a request we were honored to fulfill. As with others, we wanted to leave a memento to the victims and decided the greatest tribute we could offer would be a search dog's most prized possession: the toy they train with. Carefully, we laid Ditto's orange field dummy among the flowers at the base of the building.

The goal and purpose of FEMA search dogs is to assist in saving lives using the unique skills and abilities of the dogs. Yet, the FEMA dogs in Oklahoma City had another mission, as well. In addition to aiding in the recovery and reuniting families with their loved ones, they gave the kind of comfort and solace to rescue workers and the people of Oklahoma City that only a dog knows how to give. Likewise, the people of Oklahoma inspired the nation with their courage, strength, and hospitality in the face of incredible adversity.

∞

Barbara Naranche is the CEO of the Redlands Council of the Girl Scouts.

I drove the Girl Scout Suburban to the Myriad to deliver Hawaii's Project Aloha flowers, some coffee, and candy to the rescuers' care team coordinator. While waiting at the Myriad to make the delivery, a rescue worker, complete with helmet, coat, boots and all, came up and asked, "Are you my ride to the airport?"

"Sure."

"Really?"

"Sure, when do you need to go?"

"Right now," was the answer. Several of his team members had joined him by then.

Above: A service for the families at the conclusion of the search and rescue operation drew thousands.

— Photo courtesy of Debbie Drain

Below: A broad view of the Federal Building and 5th Street during the final stages of clean-up.

— Photo courtesy of C. W. West

I said, "As soon as I get the Suburban unloaded, I can leave." They led me into the Myriad, unloaded the Project Aloha gifts, then threw a huge duffel bag of gear in the back.

Bob, my passenger, added a two-foot-tall white teddy bear. His voice broke as he looked at me and said, "A little girl gave it to me."

Bob climbed in, and we headed for the airport. "Are you sure you know how to get there? They gave me a map." He fumbled through some papers that included his ticket along with some cards and notes from children. I assured him we didn't need a map.

"We got in yesterday. I've been up twenty-four hours. We had to get all our clearances, all our tickets." He pointed to the tags hanging on his jacket and around his neck. "My crew is going into the building tonight and I should be there, but I can't reach my wife and we've had a death in the family. I have to go home. I can't believe you're taking me to the airport just because I asked."

I said, "Bob, anyone in that parking lot or on that street would have taken you. All you had to do was ask."

He remained quiet for several minutes. "We were planning to pay our own way here, but the airlines wouldn't let us. They flew us free. We couldn't make connections in Dallas, so we decided to rent a car and drive, but when the airlines found out they arranged a connecting flight. On board people tried to give us money. One man put a $50 bill in my hand. I gave it back." He said this incredulously.

We arrived at the airport without getting lost. Bob said he'd note in his log that the Girl Scouts took him to the airport, explaining that they had to keep a log of everything. He hoisted his duffel bag, picked up his teddy bear, shook my hand, and said good-bye.

Bob was inside the airport when I discovered one of his gloves on the front seat of the Suburban. I chased him into the terminal, catching up to him at the ticket counter. "I think this is yours," I said, tugging on his sleeve. He gave me a hug in return, and I said, "Go with God."

He fingered the chains around his neck to find the cross I had noticed earlier. "I always do," he said.

Rogene Hamlin helped secure protective booties for the feet of the rescue dogs.

My friend Victoria Robinson Dunlap of Creston, Washington, called me to see if there was anything she could do to help. Vic once lived in Oklahoma, met her husband here, and every summer returns for the all-female flotilla on the Illinois River. One thing I described was the work of the search and rescue dogs and how beat up their feet were getting while working in the building. Vic said her brother, Dr. Robert Robinson of Wasilla, Alaska, could possibly help. Within thirty minutes she called me back. Robert had located 200 pairs of felt booties and was already having them transported to Anchorage for shipment. The donation had been made by mushers Lavon Barve, Joe Reddington, and Martin Buser. Vic works for Alaska Airlines, and she next set about finding a way to get the booties from Alaska to Oklahoma. In the meantime, I got in my car and went downtown to find a contact for receipt of the booties. The first roadblock I came to was manned by Oklahoma City police. Upon hearing my story, they took my home telephone number and told me they knew just the right person. I hadn't been home thirty minutes when Officer Don Browning of the Oklahoma City Canine Unit called me. I related to him what we were doing, and he gave me his mobile phone number for further contacts.

Meanwhile, Vic had been frantically trying to find transportation for the booties. Alaska Airlines offered anything and everything within their power; unfortunately, they do not fly to Oklahoma. Vic then learned that her sister from Chicago, Suzanne Robinson, was presently visiting their mother in Anchorage. Sadly, she had just had to put her beloved twelve-year-old dog to sleep. When Suzanne heard what Vic was doing, she immediately contacted Rae's Harness Shop in Anchorage. Rae's does a lot of work with the mushers. Bill Larson of that shop had been watching all the news coverage and had hoped to be able to assist in the search and rescue operation. He was the developer of a type of Cordura bootie using a material which glass and sharp rock would not cut or puncture. They got in touch with me, and I then called Officer Browning to get the number and sizes of all the search and rescue dogs in Oklahoma City at the time. As soon as Rae's received that information, they began stitching them up, with Suzanne and her mom helping. Suzanne figured it would be faster if she flew everything here herself. The opportunity to assist other dogs within hours of the death of her own dog felt very right to her.

Suzanne arrived in Oklahoma City early Sunday afternoon and, with only a thirty-minute layover, handed over to me a huge parcel of dog booties from the Alaskan mushers and Rae's, along with notes from everyone and pictures of her dog. Suzanne and I had never met, but we hugged like sisters.

I called Officer Browning, who was working the Sunday Memorial Service at the fairgrounds. He was able to break away for ten minutes and met me at a nearby parking lot. Amazingly, within twenty-seven hours of the initial phone call, I handed everything over to Don—direct from Alaska and on a weekend.

As a result, Officer Don Browning, his partner Gunny, and I, with help from Rae's Harness Shop in Alaska, are currently working on a prototype dog bootie designed specifically for search and rescue operations.

∽

Madonna Evans worked as a volunteer for the Salvation Army.

Many hours were put in over those many days and many fine people helped us put out 1,500 to 2,000 meals a day, plus snacks, to anyone who needed them. We fed twenty-four hours a day.

Bob Rogers Meat Processing donated 400 pounds of

brisket, and Bubba's Barbecue donated a smoker and the manpower to cook the meat. Junior's Restaurant in Oklahoma City and Miss Clara's Tea Room in Sand Springs, Oklahoma, both provided one evening's meals. Local Hardees and McDonald's provided breakfast almost daily. The William E. Davis Company, who lost a new employee in the blast, donated a refrigerator truck to hold donated perishables.

∽

Hal McKnight, an American Red Cross volunteer, distributed rescue supplies.

I began unloading supplies in the cold rain at 8th Street and Harvey. Since I had on rain gear, I was given a wheelbarrow and asked to haul supplies from the drop-off points. My father used to tease me as a kid by telling me, "Son, please stay away from the wheelbarrow—you don't know anything about machinery." After half a day of wheelbarrowing loads up to 400 pounds, my dad would have eaten his words.

When I first entered the freighter dock area of the building I was in a daze. We were met with huge slabs of concrete, and a large section of the north wall was completely exposed. Along the east wall were long tables holding tools and supplies. I started handing them out, from respirators to sledgehammers.

The harshness of the reality surrounding the disaster area was ever-present. This hit home early on when I unloaded several boxes containing the *Jaws-of-Life* tools. Later, I moved a free-standing blackboard from our station with the intent of posting work shifts and the names of the upcoming crews. However, after viewing the opposite side of the board, I quickly replaced it. It held the scribbles and writings from the children of the daycare center.

∽

Barry Shisler is with the USAF Reserve Fire Department at Tinker Air Force Base.

On the morning of May 5, I finished my last shift in support of the search and recovery phase at the site. Like my fellow rescue workers, I felt that virtually all hope of finding any survivors had faded. Instead of going home that morning, though, I decided to stay and help prepare for the memorial service to take place that afternoon for the rescue workers and volunteers. While working in front of the building, my attention was drawn, as it had been so many times, to a slab of concrete standing where it had come to rest during the blast. Early on, someone had painted "Bless the Children and the Innocent" on that jagged piece of cement.

Now, there were a few flowers laid nearby, a makeshift memorial to the tragedy and the tireless efforts of the rescuers. As I stood there, a city maintenance truck entered the area. It was loaded with toys, flowers, cards, and notes of thanks, all left by citizens at various street corners downtown as a tribute to the victims. The crew of the truck and I decided to add the items to the memorial at the concrete slab, and we spent the next several hours arranging flowers, cards and toys to the few tokens of love and support already there.

As we worked, a volunteer appeared and handed me a white teddy bear. Pinned to the bear was a blue ribbon sash that read, "Thank you for your efforts." Also attached was a card with a picture of an infant girl and the words, "In loving memory of Danielle Nicole Bell." The volunteer told me that the child was one of those lost in the daycare center. The bear had been brought by a relative who asked that it be placed where it could be seen by the rescue workers during the service.

That little bear had meant a lot to an innocent child. That afternoon, during the memorial service, it came to symbolize every innocent victim we had hoped to save.

∞

Catherine Alaniz's husband, Specialist Andy Alaniz, was killed in action on February 27, 1991, the cease-fire day of Operation Desert Storm. Her father, Claude Medearis, an employee of the United States Customs Service, died in the Murrah Building bombing.

I awoke to the sound of the telephone ringing in my ear. It was my cousin, Dee. She was at work in north Oklahoma City. She called to ask me if I had felt the explosion. I told her that I had been asleep and had felt nothing, and I promptly asked her what she was talking about. She informed me that a building downtown had blown up. My fiancé used to work downtown, so we have a lot of friends there, not to mention my father.

I immediately turned the television on, then called my father on his mobile, but did not get an answer. I paged him and then called his office. Nothing. I called Customs in Houston, Texas. The man there knew less than I did, but I found out while I was on the phone with him that it was the Murrah Building. I hung up with him and called my mom. No answer on her end. I became frantic! I asked my fiancé to go to her house and see what he could find out. It turned out she had been in the shower and had not been watching the news. I got up and got my two daughters dressed in record time and broke all the traffic laws on the way to my mom's house. That's where I stayed for three weeks straight. I had to be pried away from her side. After going through something very similar with my own husband, I was not about to let her find out any bad news alone.

The first night was the worst. We had an unexpected visit by United States Customs' agents dressed in their "police" coats. I saw them before my mom could tell me they didn't have any news. I lost my grip on reality and began to panic again. All the feelings I had when I found out my husband was killed in Desert Storm came rushing back with a vengeance. By the time I regained my composure, I was overwhelmed with anger. We knew there were many bodies, but they were not going to start identifying them until the next day. All we could ask was, "Why?" and all we were hearing was, "We don't know." I never thought I could make it through the first night, but with help from family and friends we managed, along with nine more nights just like it.

Six months of Desert Storm did not even compare with the emotions of the nine days following the April 19 nightmare. I'm not sure how we survived. We just did. Dad's body was recovered on April 28. We viewed him April 30, and we said good-bye to him May 2, each in our own way. I sang "Father's Eyes" at his service. My cousin played a song on his saxophone, and a few close friends and relatives filled our hearts and minds with stories of my father, stories that made us laugh, cry, and remember him the way he would have wished.

∞

Rhonda Harris is a therapist with the Fort Sill Social Work Services. She lives in Lawton, Oklahoma.

My job was to provide counseling and support for victims and fellow volunteers. Upon our arrival at the Red Cross center, we were instructed to wander about the building and offer our assistance to others. Everything seemed chaotic, people were rushing around, volunteers were coming and going; yet everyone seemed eager and determined to help. Many of the volunteers were very young, some of them teenagers. I worried about how this trauma would affect them.

My partner, Dena Putney, and I were asked to go down to the bomb site to counsel volunteers and rescue workers. The next thing I knew we were driving off in the rain with a truck full of volunteers. We arrived at the bomb site and immediately began mingling with the workers, listening to their stories. I accompanied some of them to an area of the building where bodies were being recovered. The workers were lined up and given a briefing on "bagging" the bodies. I remember one volunteer's comment about being responsible for tagging the bodies; she stood there on the corner with a shocked look on her face, a marker in one hand, and tags in the other. Then an announcement was made that the area was too dangerous to send in the volunteers and that the military would perform this task instead. Some workers seemed disappointed; they were eager to help in spite of being fearful of what they might experience.

Not long after, volunteers were once again called to begin removal of bodies. Meanwhile, my partner and I began organizing and gathering supplies for the workers. I vividly remember rushing through the aisles of supplies, all of which were covered with a sheet of heavy plastic due to the rain, and frantically trying to find the items requested: bandages, scalpels, blankets, body bags, hard hats, raincoats, and gloves. Once this task was completed I was relocated to an area underneath the building where firefighters were gathered. We spent several hours there, wandering about, talking to the workers and listening to their heart-wrenching stories.

∞

Air Force Tech Sergeant Matthew Armistead is with the 966th Airborne Air Control Squadron at Tinker Air Force Base.

Our final shift ended at 2:00 P.M. on the afternoon before the last Marine was recovered. Even though we were allowed to go home, more than half the volunteers decided not to leave until the Marine was recovered. We wanted to be there to honor him for his sacrifice. Perhaps we were looking for closure, a way to really end all the work we had been doing. After several delays, his body was recovered around 9:00 P.M. and turned over to the Marine Corps Honor Guard.

All the rescue workers stopped what they were doing as

the Honor Guard covered his body with the United States flag and escorted him away from the building. The escort was comprised of his co-workers from the recruiting office, a Marine Corps colonel, and a military chaplain. All members of the Armed Forces at the site formed a Cordon of Honor from the perimeter to the entrance of the morgue, and as the detail bearing the fallen Marine passed the members of the cordon, each member executed a slow salute. When they reached the waiting mortuary officer, the detail solemnly removed the flag and folded it into the well-known triangle that reveals only the blue field and white stars. The colonel then delivered the "Farewell to a Fallen Marine," and the chaplain offered up a prayer. The Marine was turned over to the Mortuary Affairs officer, and the detail was dismissed.

My position in the cordon had been last in line, immediately in front of the morgue. The sky above us was dark, illuminated only by the floodlights around the building. During the ceremony, the only sounds were those emanating from the generators that powered the lights. Everywhere on the site rescue workers were motionless. At a dignified pace, the escort detail made their way down the cordon, and, though the light was dim, the colors of the United States flag covering the body cut through the night like a blazing fire. The grief-stricken faces of the escort detail reminded me of the Marines who had searched the ruins of the barracks in Beirut.

∽

Suzi Shoemake is a writer and a civilian employee at Tinker Air Force Base.

A young second lieutenant was arriving for duty on the evening shift. His troops were guarding the perimeter at the site, as they had each night since the first one — two weeks earlier. They all looked young, but each had a set to his jaw that told any onlooker a lot of growing up had taken place in a short time.

Top left: Oklahoma City Police officer Kevin Thompson.
— **Photo courtesy of Kevin Thompson**
Top right: Oklahoma City Police Sergeant David Emberling with a bucket of transplanted oak seedlings.
— **Photo courtesy of Leah Taylor**
Bottom left: YMCA day care survivor Sarah Hernandez.
— **Photo courtesy of Barbara Hernandez**
Bottom right: Oklahoma Highway Patrolman Larry Dellinger with survivor Nancy Ingram of the Credit Union.
— **Photo courtesy of Larry Dellinger**

As they went to their assignments, I approached the lieutenant and requested that he consider writing about his experiences for me. I don't know which of us was more embarrassed when his eyes flooded with tears. He told me he wasn't ready to write about the things he had seen. To change the subject, I asked him where he was from. He hesitated, then told the empty space to my left, "I'm from here," he said, as tears rolled slowly down his face. "I knew when I came into the Army that I would probably go to war some day . . . I never thought that my first war would be in my own home town."

$$\infty$$

Danny Clark works as an apprentice for Clark Funeral Service in Beaver, Oklahoma.

The search was called off with two victims still buried inside, after it was decided not to chance getting anyone else hurt. Suddenly, our job was over. For two weeks all we had thought about was getting this task done and going home to our families. To leave that building we had all grown to hate so much was one of the hardest things I've ever had to do. All the people on my team were in disbelief. The job couldn't be over. There were still two people left trapped—people with families waiting grievously to be reunited with them.

$$\infty$$

Air Force Captain Jose Loya organized volunteer efforts at Tinker Air Force Base.

The last Saturday at the site we had to wear heavy-duty respirators and put Vicks Vapo-Rub under our noses to help cover the stench of death. Even so, no one held back. We still wanted to help just as much as we had the first day. I worked a total of fifty hours, and if it had been possible I would have worked more. It was all so amazing.

I guess I was like everybody else. It got to me a couple of days later. I had my sleepless nights for a while. After it was finished, I never went back.

∞

Peter Teahen, of Teahen Funeral Home in Cedar Rapids, Iowa, volunteered to work at the Medical Examiner's office.

We moved carefully to avoid stepping on anything of value or into an area that could cause further damage. As we gingerly stepped from one place to another, I spotted a photo out of the corner of my eye. A lovely face was smiling back at me as I looked down through the clutter. Her smile spoke endless words. Her eyes sent a silent message. I knew immediately that this person had touched my life in a way I would never totally understand. I reached down, moved away the heavy chunks of concrete and debris, and gently picked up the photo. As I held the glossy paper image, I tried to imagine what she was like, listening for a voice I would never hear. Her image and smile spoke of a woman who had enjoyed life and shared her joy with others. Then some heavy equipment stretched its mechanical arm somewhere below me, gingerly struggling to uncover her grave site. As we continued through the building, I carried her picture with me.

Another unforgettable face is that of a woman who responded in a selfless way minutes after the explosion, giving aid and comfort to the injured and trapped. The hurt and grief showed clearly on her face, as she recounted her anger at being forced to evacuate for two hours because of a second bomb scare. She told me of the pain that tore at her when she returned to find that the man she had left behind had died during her absence. I felt honored, days later, to stand beside her in silence when she returned to place a rose and her tears where he had died.

I remember also the face of the man who escorted me

237

through the building. His face told of his personal pain as he gazed at a gaping hole in the floor that had once held his desk and the desks of his co-workers. He spoke of taking that day off from work and of hearing the explosion, and of how he now struggles with the loss and the memories of his fellow workers.

Finally, there is the face of a firefighter: chiseled, dusty, weary. His eyes glistened as he stood clutching a three-foot stuffed bunny rabbit and his face reflected the extraordinary effort of all the rescue personnel at the scene. Though he spoke of returning home, his countenance spoke louder of a need to try to make order out of chaos.

∞

William Masten is a captain in the Air Operations Section of the Los Angeles Fire Department.

Before I left Los Angeles County, I strapped on my mental and emotional armor. My armor is hardened by years of exposure to earthquakes, fires, flood, gang violence, and civil unrest. It is a hardening honed from years of training, education, and experience. But from the moment we landed in Oklahoma City, dressed in our armor, we witnessed a power of spirit that humbled us, an invisible glue of faith and support that knitted our hearts and souls into a common cause.

We carried their letters, buttons, pins, ribbons, stuffed animals, and flowers. At the end of ten days, our suits of armor, polished to a high luster from working beside them, were stowed away for the return journey. We felt we had attained our best because of them. And when someone asks me, "Hey, what is all this *Heartland* stuff?" I will have the grandest time explaining the essence of the people of Oklahoma. A vision of right and purpose, a vision that has been blurred for too long, for too many.

∞

PART
IV

Toward Healing

One six-year-old boy got on his knees, hugged one of the dogs around the neck, and cried quietly into the dog's fur. Then the dog turned his head and licked the boy on the nose. This brought a chuckle to the boy, as he wiped the tears from his little eyes as if to say, "I'm ready to face whatever comes."

Remarks made by President Clinton during "A Time of Healing" prayer service.

The anger you feel is valid, but you must not allow yourselves to be consumed by it. The hurt you feel must not be allowed to turn into hate, but instead into the search for justice. The loss you feel must not paralyze your own lives. Instead, you must try to pay tribute to your loved ones by continuing to do all the things they left undone, thus ensuring they did not die in vain.

∞

Reverend George Back is dean of St. Paul's Episcopal Cathedral, two blocks north of the Murrah Building.

Stories were circulating. This person's friend was missing, that person's co-worker had a child in the daycare, and someone else had received 200 stitches. When the stories came to a pause, people looked away. They locked their lips. Something was flowing through the group, and it could not be stopped. It forced its way out of the eyes and down the cheeks.

There was something special about those tears, especially for the children: like Rachel weeping for her children, unable to be comforted. At an overflow chapel service, tears moved quietly like a tide through the congregation. We left washed. Anger and vengeance and anxiety and fear were flooded away for a moment and our souls were pristine and fresh.

One of the first donations we received was from a Moslem physician. His community had been faced with much hostility since the first reports connected mid-easterners with the bombing. We were contacted by Moslems, Jews, Buddhists, and many other non-Episcopalians.

We displayed both the national and state flags in our services until Memorial Day. Though the separation of church and state abides as a wise policy, our state was hurt, grieved, and wounded and we sought to affirm our solidarity with all who had been pierced to the soul by this devastating event.

∞

Kathryn Sanders is the mother of Terry Sanders, son-in-law of bombing survivor James Carver.

The day of the bombing I closed my business to be with my family. The next day when I opened, customers came in to express their sorrow and to talk. We all needed to talk.

One elderly woman, who lives alone, said that when she heard the explosion she went outside to her bus stop. She thought it was the end of time, and if she was going to die, she wanted to be with other people.

People needing people.

∞

Randy Dunn is the uncle of Karan Denise Shepherd, who worked for the Federal Employees Credit Union.

Karan worked as a loan officer for the credit union on the third floor. Her back was to the glass on the north side toward the east end of the building. Karan's section was demolished from the roof down. It just disappeared.

Although there were survivors from the credit union found the first day, rational thinking told us it would take a miracle for Karan to be found alive. Still, our hearts refused to believe the obvious. We would not let Karan go.

Throughout the first three days and nights, we held a constant vigil, praying and believing that everything would be all right. Karan's father stood a silent watch, alone just outside the Murrah Building, ready to assist however he could. Others remained at home with Karan's husband, children, and mother . . . waiting for a call.

On Saturday, April 22, a steady rain fell. The run-off slowed the rescue effort. It also began to wash away our hopes. For the next week our faith and physical strength was tested.

During that time our prayers changed. Prayers that once were for Karan's safety now became prayers that we would just be able to find her. Eventually, some of us had to rely on the strength and prayers of others. It seemed we had run slowly out of prayers of our own as numbness took over.

On April 30, Karan was finally found. Strangely, a sense of relief mixed with the indescribable sorrow. Our hearts were broken, but we knew we were at last getting Karan back and that we would finally have closure. We knew that Karan was at peace.

∽

Rockie J. Yardley is a bomb disposal technician with the Edmond, Oklahoma, Police Department.

I was assigned to the "bucket brigade." I found parts of the Ryder truck. If anybody had told me we were going to move that building in five-gallon buckets in two years, I would have laughed. We got through it in two weeks.

∽

General Kenneth Eickmann is commander of the Oklahoma City Air Logistics Center and is the installation commander for Tinker Air Force Base.

One of my biggest challenges was keeping 22,000 employees from converging on the rescue sites to help.

∽

Above: A police Honor Guard leaves a bomb site service for law enforcement victims. **— Photo courtesy of David Allen**

Below: A sheltered street corner memorial at a nearby intersection was one of many in the downtown area.
— Photo courtesy of David Allen

Dr. Leah Taylor is program director at the Moore Family Institute, a mental health and counseling facility. She helped counsel family members after the blast.

David Emberling has been an Oklahoma City cop for twenty-two years. Before that he was attached to the Army's Special Forces in the far east. He has encountered ugliness of all kinds: death by violence, horrifying injuries, destruction, immorality, and brutality beyond imagination.

I asked him, "What do you see when you close your eyes?"

He answered, "What I see, for some reason, is the image of some oak tree seedlings growing in the flower bed on the south side of the Murrah Building. I'm afraid that when the building is demolished, the seedlings will be destroyed. It keeps coming back to me that this is something I want to do — take a young oak tree and plant it in my yard, take care of it, and help it grow. Do you think it would be possible to do that?"

Amid the enormity of recent events, the oak tree seedlings had gone unnoticed by most observers. Considering the human wreckage, the seedlings were incidental. However, with the survivors rescued from the building, those tiny trees were all that remained alive in the scene of death and destruction.

Oaks are strong, magnificent, hardy survivors of adversity. They symbolize endurance, faith, and hope. Planted as a tribute, they can evoke strong feelings.

I got on the phone and called Mary Caffery, executive director of the Tree Bank Foundation, to see if she could get permission for Sergeant Emberling to take the seedlings. Permission was granted. On the sunny Saturday morning before the building's demolition, I accompanied Mary Caffery, Sergeant Emberling, and his wife, Carol, to the building site. Under the watchful eye of an ATF agent, we harvested forty-eight oak seedlings for Sergeant Emberling and his fellow officers.

Fragile and innocent, the little trees had started their lives in a place of reckless and ill-begotten ruin. They had witnessed much in their infancy—enough death, agony, and injury for a lifetime. At the homes of the police officers, these trees will enjoy the companionship of young people, friends, and family, while providing solace and respectful remembrance.

ॐ

Deborah Pippin wrote this tribute for Christy Rosas, one of the two Federal Employees Credit Union employees whose bodies were not recovered until after the implosion.

After hearing about the bomb, my family and I hurried downtown to find Christy. She had only begun her job there on April 10, and we were not familiar with exactly where the Alfred Murrah Building was located. Our first stop was St. Anthony Hospital. The streets downtown had already been blocked off, but as we neared the hospital, we could see what was left of the building in the distance. I was appalled. The atmosphere was eerie.

Hundreds of people jammed St. Anthony's. Volunteers were already in place to assist with inquiries from families and friends searching for loved ones. I remember sitting in a chair toward the back of the room and watching the activity around me. There was panic, disbelief, and horror on every face. I remember feeling as if I was not actually one of them, but only observing this desperate scene.

In the weeks to follow we settled into a macabre routine. During the day, we would get dressed early and be ready to leave in a moment's notice. We did not want to keep Christy waiting any longer than necessary. We never left the house unless the phones were covered.

The First Christian Church soon became our place of refuge. A special bonding took place there. You looked for familiar faces daily, and when a family was no longer present, you assumed they had received word and their weary wait was over.

Friday, May 5, we were told that Christy was one of the two women not found. We already knew that, without a miracle from God, Christy would not be found alive. We were not prepared to hear that she could not be found.

That morning we requested to be taken to the Murrah Building. We were escorted inside to column 22, the place where it was assumed Christy would ultimately be found. To think that we were possibly only a few feet away from her but unable to reach her was horrifying.

As we left, we met with individuals involved in the search and rescue. We could see the guilt each one of them carried for what they felt was a job not completed. Each one apologized for not finding Christy. Tears engulfed all of us. We tried our best to reassure these brave men and women that we knew, beyond the shadow of doubt, that everything humanly possible had been done to find and remove Christy from the building. This special team purchased three doves, which they planned to release: one in memory of the children, one for Christy, and one for Ms. Thompson, the other woman not recovered. Together we released a beautiful dove in memory of Christy. It was a moment I cannot begin to describe, nor will I ever forget.

∽

Kathy Graham-Wilburn and her daughter Edye Smith were at work downtown when they heard the explosion. Edye's two children, Chase and Colton, both died in the daycare center.

After the blast Edye and I went out to see what had happened. As we ran up the sidewalk glass fell in front of us and behind us. Someone yelled, "Get in the street!" We ran and ran until we were out of breath, then stopped for a second to catch our wind. We heard more explosions, which turned out to be the cars in the parking lot. To me it sounded like the end of the world.

Edye kept saying, "My babies, my babies." When we saw the building, I knew the babies were dead, but I kept lying to her, saying, "It's going to be all right." We went to Children's Hospital, where some of the children had been taken. People kept saying, "It's going to be all right." It made me so mad, and then I thought, "That's what you were just doing to Edye a minute ago."

Edye and the babies lived with us. Edye was so good to share them with us. They were my babies, too, and I just don't think that I can suffer any greater. The boys were a blessing to our home. I can't look back with any regrets. We couldn't have done anything more to make their lives better. They had the best possible life. And I wouldn't want to turn the clock back and never have had them. It was better to have had them even a short time than never at all.

∽

Robert Lastowski is employed by the United States Postal Service.

On April 28, 1995, we were working at the refreshment table located outside the damaged Center City Post Office at NW 5th and Harvey. At approximately 3:00 P.M. an out-of-state rescue worker came to the table for a soft drink. He took a crumpled dollar bill from his pocket and showed it to us. He said that he had been trying to spend that dollar since he first arrived, but his efforts had been unsuccessful. He was still amazed by that. He then thanked us and all the other volunteers for making everybody's job easier.

∽

Army Specialist Janis Levonitis is with the Public Affairs Office at Fort Sill, Oklahoma, and a writer for The Canoneer.

I spent about a week in Oklahoma City after the bombing. I was there with a colleague to chronicle the disaster and its aftermath. We saw firefighters from all over the United States, as well as FBI agents, ATF agents, and representatives from various other agencies. They have been mentioned at almost every memorial and prayer service, yet very little had been mentioned about the military involvement. I saw people from the Army, Air Force, Navy, and Marines, as well as Department of Defense civilians, working in almost every area at the site. Dozens of airmen and soldiers worked tirelessly to find even one person alive within the ruins.

The Defense Coordination Office provided military supplies to the rescue teams. They also provided body bags, wet weather gear, and other equipment. Soldiers were constantly on the phone to ensure that the workers' needs were met quickly and efficiently.

The Casualty Assistance Office worked with the Medical Examiner's office, and grave registration people from Fort Lee also assisted.

Civilians and soldiers from Fort Sill, Tinker Air Force Base, and Oklahoma National Guard and Reserve units helped gather information to identify casualties, working every day with body after body. I was amazed at how well they all kept it together. Everything a solider should be, they were: totally professional, regardless of the situation.

The military played a vital role in Oklahoma City on April 19 and throughout the weeks that followed. I'm just a soldier from Oklahoma, but I have firsthand knowledge of what other soldiers went through here.

∽

Beryl Ward, registrar with the Episcopal Diocese of Oklahoma, worked in the Diocesan Center, which was only four blocks from the Murrah Building.

On Holy Monday Fr. Ken Armstrong from Ponca City brought a huge bundle of quilts made by the Episcopal Church Women at Grace Church for the Guild of the Christ Child. I had the quilts on the conference room table, where we had been admiring them. After the blast, the seniors who lived across the street in a three-story building came tumbling out, scared, cold and even bleeding from glass cuts. All the windows in their building had been blown out. We opened our "house" to them and had them drinking coffee and watching television when law enforcement officials ran in and told us to evacuate to 12th Street, saying there was another bomb. We had sixty or seventy infirm seniors to move, and this is where the quilts came in handy. We wrapped them around these cold, scared little ladies and loaded them up into the Bishop's van and Emily's car, while some of us ran with wheelchair-bound folk. When I saw the quilts disappearing through the door, I wondered if I would ever see them again. It was a little hard to watch, as they had just been entrusted to me. The Diocesan Center staff only saw each other as a group briefly that day at various points on Robinson Street. I never expected to see medical teams running down Robinson or bloodied children being rushed about by dazed and frightened adults, or ambulances parked bumper to bumper in front of our building. This was the day from hell.

At our staff meeting on Friday, I explained what had happened to the quilts, and Bishop Moody told me to make the story public, whether the quilts came back or not. As we were leaving the conference room, the front door opened and two young ladies from the Salvation Army came in. They had with them the majority of the quilts in a plastic bag—all clean. Over time the remainder were delivered back to us by the ladies who had been warmed by them. They wanted to thank us personally. It brought home to me that what you give away freely in love returns to you in much greater measure. Just being part of the downtown community made me proud to know I had chosen to live my life in Oklahoma.

∽

Steve Henthorn is an Oklahoma City printer and a firefighter for the United States Air Force Reserve.

So who are the real heroes of this ordeal? How about the lady who drove a golf cart for the Salvation Army, delivering drinks and snacks for the police and rescue people? This lady refused to leave, even after eighteen hours on the cart, because she still felt needed. How about the American Red Cross, Feed the Children, local food organizations, and all the churches in the area? Or the ten-year-old Cherokee Indian boy who gave his spirit bag to a Sacramento firefighter? I guarantee that bag will be part of that firefighter's equipment for the rest of his career.

ळ

Jacquetta Lair is the cousin of Oleta Christine Biddy, who was killed in the explosion.

Firemen were digging frantically in the area where Oleta's office was. I knew the daycare was directly above that. As I looked up, I saw a sight that will forever be with me. Where a few hours before eight floors had been, there now was only vast open space. Sheetrock hung like bed sheets in the wind. A tree stand with a coat on it was still standing on one of the remaining floors. I knew at once that the pile in front of me consisted of nine floors, and if Oleta or anyone else was still in there, it was going to be a very long time until they were found.

As I left the area to look for my truck, I fell to pieces. I had not allowed myself any time to grieve for my cousin or the others in the past twenty-six hours, and it finally broke through. All the horrors, the wasted lives, the destruction. I don't remember driving to Mom's house. When I got there I cried and cried on her shoulder, then went to bed.

I went to Oleta's house, when I was confident that I wouldn't break down in front of her husband, Hank. His faith was amazing. The area they live in was hit hard by the bombing. Four families lost loved ones, and he went to every funeral.

Many days went by. Every day we would say, "This is the day," only to be told it wasn't. I had been there. I had seen the pile that used to be the building. I knew what they were going through downtown. I tried to explain it to the other families as we sat there. Some understood. Some didn't. Most knew the struggle the rescuers faced and did not want anyone else hurt.

Words cannot explain how much the church meant to the waiting families. Exact information was given twice a day or more, if needed. The Governor and his wife were there almost every day. Celebrities came to donate their time and help ease the long wait. Cards, letters, and flowers from all over the world came in daily. Families bonded over the long hours; lives touched in ways we never thought they would.

At night we would go to Hank's house and fill them in on the findings of the day, then go home, sleep, and get up to do it all again the next day. Hank said, "Oleta will not be found until the last baby is found. That is the way she would want it." He was correct. We were told at her funeral that she was found ten feet away from the last baby found.

Oleta was recovered on the last day of the search. The whole family was at the church when they were told around 4:00 p.m., ending two and a half of the longest weeks any of us had spent in our lives. Her body was released to the funeral home and her valuables given to Hank. Her rings were a mess. Hank didn't know if he could bring himself to clean them, so I volunteered. I had smelled dead flesh before. I didn't think it would bother me. I went over to Hank's sister's garage and cleaned them. To this day I cannot get the smell of her watch and her rings out of my mind.

∞

Bill Sicard is a firefighter with Cottage Grove Fire and Rescue in Cottage Grove, Minnesota.

I'm sorry I couldn't do more, that I didn't get to Oklahoma City sooner or stay longer, and that in the time I was there I didn't accomplish enough. There isn't a day goes by that I don't think about what happened. I commend the people of Oklahoma on how well I was treated. There were many: the young lady who brought me food as I sat on the curb during down time; the cards and letters from people in Weatherford, Laverne, Edmond, and Oklahoma City that I received after I arrived back home; and the group photo and shirt from the first-grade class of Mustang Valley Elementary in Mustang, Oklahoma. That gesture from those kids and their teacher, Amy Kloth, made what I thought was a hard-nosed firefighter with twenty years service break down and weep. I wish the people of Oklahoma could have read those letters.

∞

Firefighter Stephen Davis was left deeply affected by his involvement at the bomb site.

In the days that followed the rescue efforts, I found myself compelled to search the obituaries to see if I recognized any of the victims I helped retrieve. I'm not sure exactly why I did that. Maybe it was because I needed to learn about their lives, to connect with them in some way.

My wife, Tami, and I have worked through this together. It has helped us both to share our feelings. Sometimes just holding someone and letting them cry is enough to start the healing. Tami says God doesn't give you any burdens you can't bear, but the loss of so many lives that day seems to me a mighty burden for those left behind.

∞

Lisa Hale and her husband Jeff wrote the following letter to their infant niece in tribute to

252

Above: An aerial view of the Murrah Building and nearby Regency Tower at dawn on the morning of the implosion.
— **Photo courtesy of Oscar Johnson**

Right: Observers wait for the implosion that will bring down the building for good.
— **Photo courtesy of Hugh Scott, Jr.**

her father, Scott Williams, who died in the
bombing before she was born.

Dear Kylie Nicole,

Before you were born, your life was changed forever. The daddy you waited to see for nine long months was taken from you and the rest of your family. You will never know him personally, but his memory will live forever.

He was so excited when he heard the news of you and could hardly wait until the day you were to arrive. He thanked God for you and prayed that you would be healthy. He had so many things he wanted to tell you, so many things that he wanted to teach you. He will not get that chance, because a hard-hearted, Godless man decided to play God and touch your life forever.

Your dad was a special man. You would have loved him. He had a way of making people feel good about themselves, and he could light up a room with a funny story, a joke, or just a stupid look. He loved life and life loved him. He was a Christian man, and he set goals to put God even higher in life. So when you're old enough to understand, don't grieve for your dad, because he is beside God right now enjoying Heaven and all its riches.

We did many things together with your dad. We played golf, softball, and Sega. He was so competitive and he hated to lose. He talked many times about how he would teach you these things and how he wanted you to have that same competitive spirit. Those same desires could also be seen in his eyes when he talked about your mom, Nicole. He loved her with a passion and would do anything for her. It was definitely love at first sight. He would have been that way with you, too.

Your dad did many things in his short life. He lived life to the fullest. He did more at twenty-four than most people do in a lifetime. He visited two of his favorite places in the world — Wrigley Field, home of the Cubs, and Texas Stadium, home of the Cowboys. Those were his two biggest loves. But we know he would have traded it all just to see you and hear you say "Daddy" for the first time.

We know it will be hard for you not to be bitter, and we hope one day you will understand that sometimes through tragedy and death there are miracles. That miracle is you. You are just a child but you carry a piece of your daddy that will help many people heal. You will always remind us of how important Scott was to us and you will help us remember that Scott did many great and wonderful things in his life. And you were one of them.

With love, Your Aunt and Uncle, Jeff and Lisa Hale

∞

Louise Nakvinda lives in Enid, Oklahoma, seventy-five miles northwest of Oklahoma City.

During the weeks after the tragedy, many people were planting trees in memory of the victims. A man in Alva, seventy miles away, was digging in his front yard to plant a seedling when he found an Enid High School ring, dated 1944. With some effort they located me using the initials on the ring and an old yearbook. I lost that ring one week after graduation night, fifty-one years ago. I'm wearing it now.

∞

From the family of John Karl VanEss.

John had always said throughout the years, "When I die, plant a tree and have a party." We will do the tree . . . maybe later we will have the party.

∞

Thomas Webb is a member of the Oklahoma Section of the American Radio Relay League.

This excerpt is adapted from ARRL's **Section Leader.**

Our amateur radio operators established an emergency coordination network to help with the effort. We remained in twenty-four-hour operation until the end of the recovery effort. During the first few hours, the telephone circuits were jammed, and we were able to provide vital emergency communications to rescue and relief organizations.

Volunteer ham operators worked at the five Salvation Army canteens and headquarters, the Red Cross command post, and the primary search and rescue command post. Our operators at the Salvation Army also processed "health and welfare" inquiries from friends and relatives. Our network became operational at 9:15 A.M. on April 19 and stayed that way until 4:00 P.M. on May 2. More than 330 amateur radio operators supported the operation, working over 5,500 hours. Now, the new question about any such effort in amateur radio circles all over the country is, "Does this meet the Oklahoma standard?"

∞

Reverend Samuel Craig is pastor of Mid-Del A.M.E. Church. He served as a pastoral counselor for families of the victims.

So much death, so much pain, so many tears, and so many funerals. I attended the funeral of the Coverdale brothers on April 25 at the True Vine Baptist Church. Aaron was five years old and Elijah was two years old. The Reverend Jesse Jackson was in attendance and called our attention to the fact that Aaron and Elijah had done something no one else could do. By their deaths, he said, they had brought all of us together in one place: black, white, rich, and poor.

∞

William R. Young *is the public information officer for the Oklahoma Department of Libraries.*

For almost six years, the ODL Public Information System has corresponded with Mr. Tsutomu Saito of Sapporo, Japan. Mr. Saito is a schoolteacher and a member of the local library council in his community. When we retrieved our mail on May 10, we were pleased to see that another letter from Mr. Saito had arrived. Unfolding his letter, we found three crisp United States ten dollar bills. Our first thought was that, once again, Mr. Saito was trying to pay us for his subscription. Our newsletter is free. However, a few lines into the letter, it was evident that Mr. Saito had other plans for the money. He wanted to help. Mr. Saito is not a wealthy man and his contribution of thirty dollars almost brought us to tears. This is a copy of that letter:

Dear Sirs:
    As one of the readers who have been reading ODL, I would like to express my most sincere and deepest sympathy for the disaster of the city house building breakdown.
    I would like to send them one of my pocket money for saving the helped people! Also, there would come again the peaceful and splendidly smiling people's faces on every street inside Oklahoma and USA (and all over the world) to overcome the disaster!
                 With the best wishes, T. Saito, Japan

ഗ

Marc Bentovoja *is a captain with the Sacramento City Fire Department and a member of FEMA's California Task Force 7, Urban Search and Rescue.*

What continues to haunt me is the guilt of not being able to provide the people of Oklahoma with what I was sent there to do: give back a loved one or a child to their family.

257

After six days of disappointment, our task force was replaced, and on the seventh day we went home.

I have three children. The youngest is three years old. One day when she is old enough to understand, I will explain to her all this madness. But for now she won't have the answers when she asks why daddy sometimes cries while reading letters and why daddy hugs her so tight.

To the people of Oklahoma, I'm sorry! I wanted so much to help reunite a family, to put a child back in the safety of a parent's arms, and to let another daddy hold his little girl tight again. Intellectually, I understand that just trying may have helped someone, but emotionally . . .

To the people of Oklahoma: Thank you for showing me the real meaning of compassion. Daily, when I called home, I'd tell my wife and children, "I may not be there at home, but I'm surely with family."

⚭

Major Ronald J. Kerley is the director of Corrections and Missing Persons for the Salvation Army.

One batch of homemade cookies was supplied by a family whose daughter was deaf. They were made in the shape of a hand signing "I love you."

Other sources of comfort to volunteers and family members were the rabbits, the dogs, and Charlie the monkey. One six-year-old boy got on his knees, hugged one of the dogs around the neck, and cried quietly into the dog's fur. Then the dog turned his head and licked the boy on the nose. This brought a chuckle to the boy, as he wiped the tears from his little eyes as if to say, "I'm ready to face whatever comes."

⚭

Laura Boyd, Ph.D., is a member of the
Oklahoma House of Representatives and
a licensed professional counselor.

The evening of April 27 will always stand out in my mind. A debriefing of 200 victims and family members, which I was coordinating, was attended by a journalist, Sam, of *Time Magazine.*

Thank you, God, that Sam was there. In addition to getting a story, Sam shared his sense of compromise, intrusion, and conflict. Earlier that day, Sam interviewed the mother of Baylee Almon, the one-year-old child whose picture in the arms of the firefighter was seen around the world. That same day he visited the critically injured in hospitals and talked with families awaiting word of the recoveries of loved ones still trapped.

Sam felt invasive and mercenary amidst our pain. Little did he know how critical to our recovery was the need to tell the stories of love and loss, of terror and courage, of life and death. Until we can exhaust our need to tell and our need somehow to write our own renditions of "what and why," Sam, and the countless other nameless saints like him, will be a gift to help us all heal.

ᗧᗩ

Jon R. Wallace is director of Social Emergency
Services for the Tulsa Area Command of the
Salvation Army.

I was sitting in a restaurant along I-35 with Mr. Wilcoxson one evening. I was wearing my soldier's uniform, and he was wearing his identification badge. A man walked up to our table and snatched our ticket from right before our eyes. We had never seen him before. After asking some questions, we discovered the man had been scheduled to go to the Social Security Office in the Murrah Building on the morning of the bombing. He failed to keep his appointment, which had been for 9:00 A.M. He heard us talking about our efforts with the Salvation Army and determined that he was going to buy our dinner.

∽

Robert S. Daniels is a lieutenant in the Salvation Army. He worked at a canteen at 5th Street and Oklahoma.

Each night the same men dug through the rubble. Each night the same medical personnel stood by, hoping to be able to help a survivor. Each night the same agents monitored the building, keeping it safe for the rescuers.

These men and women hoped when hope lay buried under tons of steel and concrete. They would not leave until every person was accounted for. They did not see bodies. They saw people. They saw families agonizing over missing loved ones and children hoping to see their mothers and fathers again. They saw life in the midst of massive death.

These are the men and women who closed their eyes to visions of mangled bodies and torn families. They are the real unsung heroes.

∽

Army Brigadier General Leo Baxter is assistant commandant of the Field Artillery School at Fort Sill, Oklahoma.

I've watched the people of Oklahoma since April 19, watched how they've acted, watched a tearful, proud, wonderful memorial service, and watched firefighters, police officers and rescue workers from all across this state come together in a celebration of life. I've learned that we must be bigger than all of this, we must overcome all of this, and we must never, never forget all of this. I've learned from watching the citizens of this rural, unnoticed, lightly populated, country-western state full of people with traditional moral values and ideals.

It was when I learned these things I realized I, too, had become an Oklahoman. And when I became an Okie, I discovered some truths. I realized anew that blood is red, just as skin is black, white, yellow, and brown. The truth is, in times such as these, what matters is the bleeding, not only from the body but from the soul. Skin color doesn't matter. I wonder why we can't recognize this truth every day.

∞

Oklahoma City social worker Patty Childress volunteered at the disaster site.

When the team of Los Angeles volunteers left, they said farewell by singing "Oklahoma" to the new friends they were leaving behind. They didn't know all the words, and the tune was a little off. In fact, it sounded like it was being sung in rounds. Suddenly, their rescue dog began to sing along. His trainer tried everything to get the dog to stop, but he was determined to go on with the show. It was the most beautiful rendition of our state song I've ever heard.

∞

Paul Myers is a veterans employment representative with the Oklahoma State Employment Services.

The first Saturday after the bombing, I was in Jonesboro, Arkansas, 400 miles east of Oklahoma City. I had driven all night, and my only thought was to find a cheap motel and get a few hours sleep before heading on to Oklahoma.

I pulled into a convenience store for another cup of

261

coffee. While I was standing at the cash register, a woman hurried into the store and asked, "Who owns that little red car out front with the Oklahoma tags?"

Hesitantly, I raised my hand. "I do," I said.

The woman walked up to me and stood there for a moment, her eyes filling with tears. Suddenly, she wrapped me in a hug. "Take this back to Oklahoma with you," she whispered in my ear.

Since the bombing, I had kept myself strung as tightly as a barbed-wire fence. I hadn't cried when I saw my friend Stan in the hospital. I hadn't cried when I stood in front of the building and viewed the destruction firsthand. I hadn't cried when I pinned blue ribbons on my wife and children to honor the dead niece and grand-nephew of a friend. But there in the arms of a stranger, 400 miles from home, I cried.

I took that hug back to Oklahoma City and gave it away dozens of times over the next several weeks. There was plenty to go around. In fact, I still have some of it left, just in case anyone needs it.

∽

Carrie Hulsey covered the disaster daily for KTOK radio.

I guess the most memorable moment for me was after the memorial service at the building for the fire and police people. As the searchers and volunteers were walking out, a crowd of people gathered outside the barricades and began applauding. Those sounds of cheering and applause are burned in my memory as vividly as the sound of the bomb.

∽

Mary Lou Washburn's husband, Raymond, who has been blind since childhood, operated the

Above: Several thousand spectators watched in awe as the Federal Building fell the morning of the implosion.
— **Photo courtesy of Oscar Johnson**

Below: The moment of the building's final destruction.
— **Photo courtesy of David Allen**

fourth-floor snack bar inside the Murrah Building.

I always thought that when a loved one was in a life or death situation I would be able to tell, or feel, if he was alive. I didn't know that morning. From all the reports I had heard coming out of downtown that morning, I thought he couldn't possibly be alive.

When I got to the downtown area, I parked and tried to run up to the building, but I was stopped. I went home and called my office, thinking that if he were alive he would try to call me at work. I was told that St. Anthony Hospital had left a message. Raymond was there.

I'm more appreciative of life now. It's a miracle that Raymond or anyone else got out alive. We take it day by day and are more thankful of each other now. The memorial service was the start of our healing.

This tragedy has drawn people together. I got a call from a stranger in Reno. She was sad and just wanted to talk with someone from Oklahoma. An operator connected her to me. We talked and she asked for my address, because she wanted to send a card. She sent the card and in it was a check for $100. Raymond received Braille letters from kids at an institute for blind children in New York.

That's the good I see out of this. Besides the evil in mankind, it has shown the goodness of mankind.

∞

Survivor Ernestine Clark of the main library continues to be involved in the downtown community.

On Sunday, October 29, six months after the bombing, a special and unexpected event took place downtown that, for me, was a healing experience. The Sunbow Walkers, mostly Native Americans from the East Coast, came through Oklahoma City on their walk from Massachusetts to California. Our church was asked to serve them dinner, and it was announced that they had been given permission to go to the site and conduct a special prayer ceremony.

I wanted to go, even though I would be on one side of the fence, and they – the walkers, Medicine Men, and others – would be on the other, saying prayers for that bloodied ground. They walked from Wylie Park all the way up Robinson to the site. We could hear their drums from a distance, and as they neared I shifted with others to the corner. A minister I knew was part of the procession, and as they passed by he reached out and quickly pulled me into the group just as it rounded the corner to enter the gate that had forbidden entry to everyone since April 19.

For the first time I walked onto the site. For the first time I felt the uneven, recently-laid grass squares beneath my shoes. Immediately the grief welled up in a river of pain, squeezing the breath out of me until the tears fell, rolling down my face, unstoppable and unashamed.

We were told to form a circle, and after a prayer we sat down. The ceremony was long. Some of it I was familiar with, like the sage cleansing of us all – a "smoking" ceremony that was performed not just once, but three times. Then the inner circle, consisting of the Medicine Men, began a separate smoking ritual, using words kept secret from the rest of us.

While they made their various oblations to the earth, sky, and four corners, I looked down at the grass beneath me and stretched out my fingers to feel it. It was turning brown now, as if dying. More tears. So many lost lives. So much wishing they had been found alive. Wishing it so hard that the heart and mind ached most terribly. To my right, in the circle, a Native American walker sat with his head bowed. To my left, an African American lady wept quietly, her tears matching mine. We said nothing, but joined hands for the final prayers. We then stood and hugged, not letting go for a minute or two.

I looked again at the earth, covered with that uneven blanket of grass, now thinking that anything was better than the raw dirt and hellish hole it replaced. The wall that had

This symbol of unity and hope on a downtown building could
be seen for miles.
— Photo courtesy of David Allen

formerly attached the vanished Federal Building to its parking garage stood in mute and scarred testimony. I turned and went home.

∞

Dale Kitzman is a senior probation and parole officer with the Oklahoma Department of Corrections.

I was walking south on Robinson from 6th Street. It was like walking into a tunnel. There were no lights anywhere. The blackness was unlike any I had ever experienced. A steady drizzle dripped against the broken glass still piled along the curbs, and the hulks of boarded-up buildings lined empty sidewalks.

A raw, cold wind blew against my back, and I lifted my head to turn up my collar. It was then that I saw it: a huge cross lighting the north side of a downtown skyscraper. Whatever happens, I thought, we're going to be okay.

Index to Reference Copy